NEWS FROM WANDALAND

NEWS FROM WANDALAND

KODELL PARKER

To order additional copies of this book, contact:
Xlibris Corporation
1-888-795-4274
www.Xlibris.com
Orders@Xlibris.com
80467

CONTENTS

America's Independence Day.. 9

Celerating The 4th Of July 11

America An Unfinished Nation 13

Memorial Day 17

Innocence Lost.. 21

Changing Times 23

Making Memories... 27

Reflections Of Days Gone By 30

Big Doings At Wandaland.. 35

Traditions 37

The Big Clan Gathering 41

Thanksgiving Day 43

Self Improvement... 45

On Running The Mouth 48

Don't Argue With Idiots.. 53

Teaching An Old Dog New Tricks 55

On Relationships... 59

Keeping Up Appearances.. 62

Moving On Up To The West Side... 64

Hindrance To Life 68

Inventions... 69

A SeNtimental Journey... 73

A Visit To The Doctor 75

Just Hanging Out.. 77

Stop The World And Let Me Off... 80

Spreading The Wealth 82

Solicitations.. 84

Telemarketer.. 87

Brain In Depression 89

London Leaves Are Falling 92

Henley Our Cook 95

Geese In Formation 97

Necked As A Jay Bird 100

Halloween 102

The High School Year Book 106

No Underwear For Birthday 110

Casting Pebbles In The Water 112

Sitting On Wally World's Bench 114

Lye Soap 117

Friendly People 119

John Whitaker Store At Lilbert 123

Columbian Bean Man 126

Sugar Daddy 128

Cajun Coffee 130

Forwarding E-Mails 133

Thrilling Days Of Yesteryear 136

Replacing My Engine Valve 138

The Reminiscence Magazine 141

The Last Trail Ride 144

09/10/2008

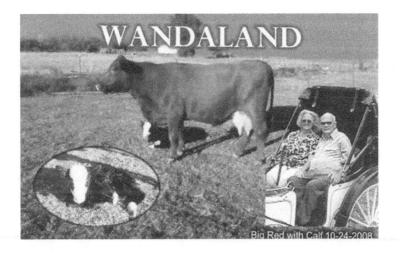

WANDALAND

Big Red with Calf 10-24-2008

AMERICA'S INDEPENDENCE DAY

Hello folk hither and yonder, you have mail from Wandaland where the cows are always hungry and don't give milk.

Many countries have an independence day, a day to commemorate their independence from another country. It may be known as Independence Day, as a date or by a different title. It is a date in history to remember when their Declaration of Independence occurred. This declaration is a proclamation usually written. The declaration of independence could very well precede the independence in actuality or it may be declared as a result of gaining independence.

Various kinds of celebrations are corporate and some are.private, with many becoming a tradition. It is a natural instinct to celebrate many things, e.g. birthday, anniversaries and even "Ground Hog Day" in some locals. While in the United States there are a number of federally recognized holidays (bank holidays). Within reason everyone is free to celebrate according to their own dictates. Independence is mostly about freedoms, primarily that of self government, discipline and self reliance. According to the Holy Bible all people exists (or should) as independent persons with the freedom of choice. The belief is extremely strong in the U.S. that all people should have the choice of government as well as many other freedoms of choice.

In A.D. 1620 people from England came to parts of North America to settle in a new land. Eventually there became 13 colonies, which later became the 13 original states of the United States of America. On July 4, 1776 the people of this new country declared its independence from England. This independence was desired as a freedom from taxation and to several highly important issues. About 10 years after the "Declaration of Independence", in A.D. 1787 the document on how this new nation would be governed (The Constitution of the United States) was enacted.

The U.S. Constitution (verb & noun) has 7 original articles with 27 amendments. It also contains a "Preamble", a statement, a thesis, of what the articles and amendments are about, so to speak, It may be said the Preamble states forth the governing principles of how this nation government will be for and by the people of the Union. It is believed the U,S, Constitution has lasted longer than any other. in the world.

An Anthem is a song or musical score used to tell about a tradition, a struggle, achievement, life, etc. In a sense it is a eulogy, although that is generally ascribed to a person. Various schools, colleges, universities and clubs have anthems. Christianity in the U.S. has an anthem generally accepted as "The Battle Hymn of The Republic." There are state and national anthems. The United States National Anthem is the song "Star Spangled Banner; the lyrics first being a poem to speak about the struggle (a battle) of war for independence. (I believe England's National Anthem to be "God Save the Queen/King." The United States of America has an unofficial National Anthem which is "God Bless America,"

Of little doubt many people have their preferred way of celebrating the various things celebrated. Culture probably has a tremendous influence on how an event is celebrated, and such may also be a tradition. People's birthdays and marriage anniversaries are celebrated according to individual preferences. The same can be said about national holidays as well.

As eluded, celebration of various things here in the U.S. is indeed "The American Way", but most if not all, the ways an event is celebrated can not be said as "The American Way." But perhaps it can when we consider the actual "American Way" is freedom of choice.

The celebration of New Years' Day and the 4th of July with firework displays has about became an "American Way", to celebrate but certainly not the only American Way.

To enter into a contest of how many hotdogs I could eat in ten minutes just isn't my cup of tea. I am indeed grateful to live in a country where people can do just that, or what so ever meets their fancy. Yep, it all about independence, freedom to choose how to celebrate Independence Day; a day which allows personal independence as well as freedom from being taxed without a say in the matter Independence, to what ever extent enjoyed, however it may be viewed should not be misused, or taken for granted as an entitlement, even though that be the case. It should be revered as a privilege which needs be guarded. Independence each of us has chosen as our own "American Way" of life in so many things can be lost through neglect and abuse. It doesn't take much to rethink the matter but maybe a little more to repent.

I can hardly wait until next New Year! Or wait for my next birthday or to celebrate on a day to commemorate the advent of Peanut Butter and Jelly Sandwiches. These are a few of the things being plundered on the last few days here at Wandaland where the cow are always hungry and Ole Patch, the Blue Tick Hound, is the only animal who will eat people food, even a PB & J sandwich. Kp

CELERATING THE 4TH OF JULY

Hello rowdy friends, cousins, and all others on the top and bottom sides of the world. It is mail call time from Wandaland where the cows are always hungry and never gets mlked.

We the people of the United States in North America will be celebrating our independence in just a few days. The French helped the struggling 13 colonies gain independence and the declaration was on July 4, 1776. It was about ten years later, in 1787 the states as a nation adopted the Constitution of the United States. Practically every country in the world has its independence date.

When I think of Independence Day my thoughts are carried back to a number of things. When my kids were young at home it was a tradition to have lemonade from fresh squeezed lemons with seeds and pulp floating in a gallon jug with chipped ice. We usually had hamburgers and hot dogs that day as well. Later on, light years ago when I was working for British Petroleum on American Soil (Alaska) there was no formal recognizing of the day, however in later years there was.

Independence Day, the 4th of July reminds me of a time being in "boot camp" of the Navy. We were taught the values of what the "grand old flag" stood for, and to stand at attention and salute it when it passed in review. Also at all other time when it was being hoisted and lowered and when the National Anthem is being played. Proud Americans don't just salute the flag without remembering.

When I see public service people and others people as Policemen, Fireman, Medical Personal and others wearing a flag patch on their uniforms I am reminded how fortunate I am to be born in this country and have the freedoms and prosperity we have There are numerous others as cub scouts, boy scouts, girl scouts, 4-H club and some sports who proudly wear the American Flag. Lest we should forget, freedom is not free; there have been many different kinds of prices paid for it. There is always present a danger there will not be "Stars and Strips Forever" may God forbid!

I sometime wonder what life was like back in the 1700's when there was wild turkey, when rivers were not damn and polluted, the air was fresh and clean. When much of the world was not cemented over and huge trees grew in the forest where squirrels live and played. It was a time when honey was taken from a hollow tree instead of a supermarket. One would have to assume there were fears in olden time, fears of many kinds. There was fear of various kinds of sickness, and fears concerning the loss of life.

A magazine ad for cigarettes a few years ago said "you have come a long way baby." I think that had to do with women smoking in public places. We have come a long way in may respects, some for the better and some for the worse perhaps. Much of life seems to revolve around synthetics instead of the "real deal." Humanity has found and developed many different ways to destroy life.

We have become prisoners with a different kind of fear. We have over indulged in much and greed, long in the making, has finally caused much anxiety with "we the people."

Recon me and my significant other will be hoofing it down to Nacogdoches County comes next Thursday evening to spend the week-end with relatives in them parts. Diane I want to mention that grandbaby is so cute. I have saved her picture, the one with a big smile. She is getting prettier by the day. We are still getting good rains often enough to keep the grass growing, While it is not the best time of the year for such, some of the cows are having calves.

On account of suffering miseries with my thinking parts, I'll just saddle up and ride on out of dodge. 'Till then when the breezes currents brings news from Wandaland where the cows are always hungry and not time to milk them, y'all keep your gun powder dry and wind to your back. Did I mention the 4th of July is also watermelon time? kp

AMERICA AN UNFINISHED NATION

The "Preamble" to the Constitution of the United States is similar to a thesis in that is sets forth what the Constitution concerns. It is a preamble and does not give any expressed or insinuated power to the Federal or State Governments. It simply state as an introduction or "overview" that which "we the people" (more precisely people of that day) approved (ordained) as a governing set of laws and rules. It has been determined and ruled by the Supreme Court that "United" was to meant to have a government "over the people of the States" rather than the States agreeing to become a union as a "more perfect union." In other words, all states are subject to all federal laws as they would be superior over state laws and neither can states decide to pull out of the "Union."

While I do not intend to say much of anything concerning what the "Courts" has determined about the Constitution, the Supreme Court has ruled the meaning of the Constitution has not changed, especially the power ordained in Article III since the day the constitution was ratified as that was challenged in the Supreme Court. Even though the complex of the nation has changed, becoming more complicated with time; the passing of time with the development of the nation has no basis for any distinction of judicial power.

In order to grasp the "preamble" to a better degree, and especially the phrase "to form a more perfect union" one only needs a small understanding of the instrument, document, decree ordered namely the "Articles of Confederation. While The Articles of Confederation did to a shallow degree unite the states, it was extremely weak and did not address all the many problems each of these states had with each other. Prior to, and during the time the Articles of Confederation were in affect each of these states had it own Constitution, Governor and people to represent them in their own local government. There is little doubt by any "political scholar" the phrase "In order to form a more perfect union" refers to the highly imperfect Articles of Confederation.

When one learns of all the conflict the first colonies had between them and later between each state and the weak Articles in the Decoration of Independence it causes one to wonder why there was not a "civil war" among these state with one to come out as the conquer. The federal government had an army and relied on each individual state to support the government with taxes it collected from people of the state.

The Articles of Confederation did attempt to bring all these self governing states together to act as one body. It is unbelievable what had been written. Each state had its own money and some states' money was worth a lot more than others. Some states had its own interstate commerce in that it charged a tariff for product coming in from other states. This situation produced a lot of hostility and counter action. The states as a Confederate had a lot of difficulty entering into treaties with other countries, and England would not indulge in commerce with the Confederate. States disputed each others boundaries, and rivers which ran through different states. There was the Indian problem which England continued to promote going against the treaty they had signed with the confederate. Each state had their own laws with respect to human law. It was like 13 separate countries wanting to form a "more perfect union" with each having its demands.

If these "little independent countries" (states) were to survive its only hope was to "form a more perfect union: and with time enact "amendment" in the process of retaining a more perfect union. It is believed, there can never be a "perfect" union for the state, but there will always be a "more perfect union" as long as one branch of the government does not take power away from the other.

It can be said perhaps with some validity that the Articles of Confederation were a "hurried up" form of government after independence had been won. There appears to be evidence of thought for a centralized government before independence was won. As mentioned it is a miracle that these independent states with no strong central government over them did contribute to the effort so that independence was won, and even survive during the days of "Confederate Articles government." So weak was the "central government" that a foreign country did occupy the land and the English did burn down the capitol before they were driven out for good.

When I think about a "more perfect union" I am reminded of the "European Union" and how much change it has made for the countries that joined. However there was a group of independent self-governed "provinces" who desired a "centralized government" so they could have a king who would go out before them and promote their general welfare, especially when it came to foreigners taking over, enslaving them and changing their "way of life."

It was a lengthy time after winning independence from England that the Constitution for a "United States" came into being. The length of time is only important in that there was no rush to not having a "more perfect union."

There were a number of "conventions" where representatives of the states met to "hammer out" a more perfect and adequate centralized laws to governing the union. There was to come a time when a very costly civil war tested remaining a union under a centralized government.

It was after the civil war that President Abraham Lincoln made what is known as the Gettysburg Address to the people such as no other President has or can make. It is my contention that most citizens of the U.S. have no awareness of this address, which is as precious as the preamble to the constitution.

I for one can not but help becoming a little emotional when I read the entire speech Mr. Lincoln made. I suppose that older Americans remember various parts but not everything said. It began with "Four score and seven years ago our fathers brought forth on this continent a new nation, *conceived in Liberty and dedicated to the proportion all men are created equal."*

There is nothing in the speech which is not "moving." It speaks of the struggle of brave men, the living and dead who consecrated what happen on that battlefield, and that it should never be forgotten. *"It is for us the living, rather, to be dedicated here to the which they fought here have thus far so nobly advanced."* And then ending with immortal statement: "that we highly resolve that these dead shall not have died in vain-that this nation, *under God* shall have a new birth of freedom, *and that of people, by the people,FOR THE PEOPLE, shall not perish from the earth."*

I like many others fellow Americans realize we have grave international concerns as well as our own domestic affairs. I can not help feeling above all other concerns it is our resolve to be a nation under God having a centralized government as in better days where it "shall not perish" due to concern. Should it perish who is it that can say I do not share the blame? Of little doubt, there will be some who will not ponder the question with introspect, that is having no self mental examination of how it happened and admitting to such grave negligence. As for me and my house we will always pray "God Bless America, the Land that I love." I believe it to be the intent of our constitution that the federal government is not to have "interfering powers" over non state established religion and that the courts got it wrong big time when it thinks Christianity has no place in government. For a moment stop and think who organized the first "places of formal learning" and especially those places of high learning as colleges and universities.

What are that institution that promotes "moral law" which many of our civil laws have derived from? Do people really care or just wish? Less than a year ago a group put actions to their words, and perhaps they will once again do more than just wish for a change in the direction this nation seem to be heading being straying form the government established by the constitution and it not perishing from the earth. Narcissistic people are not hesitant to tell the world America is not a Christian nation, but one of visions and principals. Perhaps this is true, but to not misleading they should say America is no longer a Christian nation. What they fail to communicate to the world are the words of Mr. Lincoln in the Gettysburg Address. A Narcissist person is highly self deceived in that they believe they are endowed with wisdom and seek out their on good. There is no doubt in their minds that they know what is best for every one.

This nation has been through all known tragedies to mankind, such as earthquakes, floods, hurricanes, volcanoes erupting, tornadoes and all other "acts of nature." The nation has survived all kinds of man made tragedies, the civil war, depression, and recessions, attracts upon our country, in two world wars and Lord knows what else. It has survived with the promise of God He will see those who are "under Him" through any circumstance. God does not necessarily protect from danger but see people through danger. You can take it to the bank God allows despites, the little dictators, the narcissists, Kings and Governors of the earth to be in rule. A coalition of all armies of the world is as a feather in a typhoon as opposed to the power of God.

There is a proverb which states "pride goes before a fall." By all means we should be prideful of this great and beautiful country who is the "champion of freedoms" but these "United State" must never forget its humble beginning and how it came to be so blessed. Kp

MEMORIAL DAY

Hello everyone, you have mail from Wandaland where the cows are always hungry and we never milk them/

A good many years ago Jimmy Rogers made famous a song "Time Changes Everything." There is some truth to these lyrics! Over a periods of time the "when, how and why' of Memorial Day has evolved to a day which, to a great extent, undermines its original purpose as can be seen. It, like some other days of celebration, has had it observance day changed to allow for a three day week-end of pleasure. Memorial Day formally known as "Decoration Day" was observed on May 30th of each year until it was changed to the last Monday in May to create a long week-end.

Armistice Day, later to become 'Veterans Day" was celebrated along with the original Decoration Day, but Veterans Day was move back to its original date. I believe this is in November as it commemorates the end of World Wars I and II. It was after World War II when it was changed to Veterans Day and included honoring service people who died in both wars.

Memorial Day, which in the beginning was know as "Decoration Day" has its origin back to the American Civil War. This day of honoring the war dead of the Union Army is believed to have started by a group of freed slaves who decorated their graves.

The first official day for Decoration Day was started on May 5th, 1866. It was to commemorate the fallen troops of each army. The Southern States were most reluctant to observe this date in the beginning. Most all southern states had their own Decoration Day. There was still a lot of hostility toward the North by the South and very few Union Army Veterans lived in the South. Texas' Decoration Day was known as "Confederate Heroes Day" and was celebrated in January.

Memorial Day (of this era) is a day "set aside" to commemorate men and women who have died in service of our country in all wars. The United States has become a nation which strongly believes in the freedom of all people. It is no wonder how Memorial Day first commenced; how it came to be and observed for a number of centuries. Small US flags are place on graves in the National Cemetery, and there is an official time set aside for a "moment of silence:" in Washington. The VFW and volunteers will in many cemeteries across the country decorate veterans' graves with small flags. The Sunday before Memorial Day is still observed as Decoration Day to honor those who are dead but not veterans.

The next time you see a military service person gracefully get their attention and say "Sir (or Lady) thank you for being in the service. While each may have their own reasons for enlisting, never forget they are "there for us."

It is time to happy trail to everyone from Wandaland where the cows are always hungry and don't give up their milk. kp

Wanda—Kodell Parker

Satisfied Mind

In American History there was the study of the Monroe Doctrine which stated simply hemisphere was not open for the colonization by European countries. This past presidential election has the same "overtones" and similarities as that of Andrew Jackson defeating John Q. Adams. I am left wondering if the Monroe Doctoring, as to the United States, has been allowed to be nullified without a struggle. Hello folks, you have mail from Wandaland where the cows are always hungry and never milked.

It was about one year ago when Wanda and I visited her cousin Diane in New Zealand where she told us about her granddaughter spending the summer and the wonderful time they had together. When it came time for the granddaughter to go back to her home in Australia Diane had expressed sadness she was leaving. The granddaughters said "do not be sad it is over just be glad that it happened". I don't know, but suppose that to be the perspective of many young girls in their teens.

People of my generation can say the same thing about the departure from a time and way of life we were most fortunate to have lived and had. I was born at the start of the great depression in the 1930's. (There has been more of "everything" this past seventy-five years than all the years that proceeded.) In the 30's we were poor in material thing, but so were all others we knew. One of life's most important lessons is that "things" or people can not make a person happy. That is one of a few things a person has to do for them selves. The truth is we were too happy and blessed to "take account" of being poor. There are riches and richness of another kind. As Porter Wagner sings about, there is nothing more important at the end of time than to depart with a satisfied mind knowing we, as individuals, have attempted to live rightfully.

Many unimaginable things have happen, most intended for the good perhaps and some to advance evil in the world. I can not imagine being around to experience what America will be like in 2015 but I may be granted these bonus years. If so I do not think I will be looking back and asking "what went wrong."

Many thoughts bounce about in my mind, like what happen to Adam and Eve and why such happen. Eve was deceived by evil to become wise like God. And ole Adam, well he willingly transgressed after being persuaded. Can't you just imagine Eve poking "an apple" at Adam and saying "here big boy, take a bite of my apple and you can see what a perfect 10 I am." Course we do not know exactly how it went down on account God only states "the facts."

I wonder what America has fallen in love with. Is it the various sciences or our mighty chariots? Do we have a burning desire to be like other nations? Flip Wilson made a few profound statement as "wherever you are, that's where you are." Doris Day sang a song about "whatever will be will be", and Oh yes, "the future is not ours to see." Perhaps that is the way it is supposed to be. My authorized King James Bible states "faith, hope and charity is the way to live successfully." Hope for a better tomorrow is good.

We are living in a "time" when it seems the majority of people do not believe in absolutes, but that all things are relative. Not so, and should it be then we all should throw in the towel. For what purpose is our life? Reality teaches we are here today and gone tomorrow like a blade of grass or a puff of smoke.

We desperately desire to know in this age of information. We want to know why certain things happen when we cry out otherwise. We even dare to question God why things are the way they are not realizing the wrong person is being asked. God does not violate the "free will" of mankind; otherwise He would not be the covenant Elohim (Jehovah) God of the Universes.

God places in the mind to do well and warn of consequences for disobediences, yet He is a merciful God and will heal the land IF the people called by his name will shape up. He just might do the same for America! Although said in a little different way the same promise is made to individuals. There are perhaps thousands of promises God makes to people however just about each promise has a condition to be met to be obtainable.

We do not truly know about tomorrow, and can not totally sure about today. Dear Lord, "help us today, one day at a time, show us the way and give us the strength to live as we should." So from all of us here at Wandaland where the cows are always hungry and never get milked, to all of your out there "let a smile by your umbrella on a rainy day. kp

Innocence Lost

Hello to all "out there", you have news from Wandaland where the cows are always hungry, never gets milked.

9/11 ushered in one of the greatest changes in the American way of life perhaps since the time independence was won. The recent money crisis will have some impact as well because world money is measured against the American dollar. There are things on the horizon which will make our current problem seem small. World money is linked to the American Dollar in several ways. The American Dollar, our economy, technology, and a few other factors is what has made the United States a "Super Power" The greatest ingredient of all has been God's blessing upon the United States. It is highly possible we are in the eve of a "change" which will be devastating regardless of party administration.

The world has become unstable as a bucket of water being hauled around on Loop 635 in Dallas, Texas with traffic suddenly stopping and jockeying for lanes. Our recession which has manifested it self in many ways (loss of jobs, greed, etc.) is a primary cause (as I see things) for America (the States) to loose the "Super Power" ranking among nations of the world. It appears the United Nations pushing for a "one world" finance system. When the declines of "world powers" are looked upon it is generally agreed their decline and "Super Power" loss resulted from straying away from the principals who gained them prominence in the first place.

The world has been changing at a fast pace here of late and most people, including me, has not noticed or understood the implications. It appears to me the world situation could explode as a result of several different happenings. The States is not the only nation in trouble with money or a lagging economy; however it appears we will bear the brunt of the "so called recovery" or "reinstating." I think Americans have been too busy living the "American Dream" or concerned about not becoming one of the "have not's", of when to sleep, where the next meal is coming from to see what is unfolding.

I have read over the "Recovery Bill" to come before the congress for some kind of action. Much of it I do not understand, and perhaps only might if I had a lot of time to devote to all the different aspects. I think I understand a little and not sure that I agree with what little I think I do understand. The government does not "own money" but takes money from the taxpayers (people, business, etc.) and supposedly manages it for the public good. It just seems to me the bill proposed is nothing more than giving the money "we need now" to others as our payment for the mistakes others have made for us.

A slight amount of inflations is indeed some helpful to growing an economy' but when greed causes fast growing false economy such as we have had it can only swell until it bursts wide open. Yes foreign banks bought our mortgages, many which should have never been allowed to happen, and now we are proposing to bail out these foreign banks because of the government's mistake of letting it happen. (Foreign banks buying up mortgages pumped money into the economy)

I suppose it is as much about trust in the government, especially capitalism, as anything, but it just seem a bit wrong to me. To me it goes to "personal responsibility" be it banks here or foreign, and individuals.

There is a provision in the bill if the "tax payer bail out" doesn't work, and then the "rascals" responsible for the "financial services" failure would have to "cough-up" the money. I suppose any senator or congressman who allows for such gross negligence is isolated form "coughing up." We elected the dudes, and since we can't make them pay for their own mistakes we can vote them out of office and send a message to house and senate "their party is over" as well.

Remember Mary Poppins and the "spoon full of sugar"? The bill seem to say, OK we are not sure if we can trust what we have proposed and even if we can trust those who will supposedly have oversight, so therefore we will give you 50 billion to start with. We are supposed to believe the medicine goes down a little more delightful in a spoon full at a time as to the whole bottle at once. And while that can possibly be true, it is a remedy and not a cure.

Someone has said "integrity" is doing the right thing when you don't have to. This may be a good definition and it says about the say thing as "morality can't be legislated." Greed as in gluttony at the expense of others is bad morality, and I think to many people take advantage of others simply because of "circumstances." The desire of greed is a trait people are born with. It takes a genuine "born again experience" for that desire to change and while there is a true desire there is the ever presence of temptation to yield to.

Our land, as well as others is in need of much healing so says Wandaland where the cows are always hungry and never gives up any milk. What say ye?. kp

Changing Times

Hello folks, it is time to drag up a chair and "while away" on some time with news and other "tom-foolery" on "changing times" from Wandaland where the cows are always hungry and never get milking. You might even want to pour another glass of lemonade.

We got wind a homecoming was brewing down in my ancestral land. I did a goodly amount of mulling the situation over but found a little left over space in one of the cells to park the matter in before the list of pros and cons of trucking on down was finalized. Our forgetful; Parson Man.who does most of the talking at the Sunday meeting house, was advised we would most likely be laying out that day. We have found this is the best way to keep off the backslider roll. Once you get straddled with that label you won't automatically have your name rubbed off the truancy list.

Well y'all, who are still able to roll out of bed, swallow a little grub; then float down a fist full of colored pills before heading out someplace to commence a week of fighting personal poverty know how Monday morning can be. All folks like me have to do is wallow in bed until the mood strikes then try crawling out and taking a fist full of different colored pills. To much of a good time on Sunday night hinders rolling out, limbering up and getting the smoking smoke fumigated out to the pasture before the 10 o'clock banging on the screen door erupts. It doesn't hurt anything to clear a path from the front door to the best seat in the house either. Ten in any morning is not a good time to have casual a or distinguished guest making a landing. Usually they have already started belching from to much coffee and it is a bit early in the day to have the first can of Millers. About all one can do is fake a surprise and being thankful for the visit and let stuff happen as it will.

Early Sunday morning, the woman of the house, the one who is first to crawl out and last to start wallowing in bed got up, put on a string of "rich bitch" genuine simulated pearls, got some least patched overalls out the wash someday box for me and said put these on. She said I have made up your mind (nothing unusual about that) because we are going to the homecoming. She used my own words "again" me. She done said you wonder how all the old people are doing and what they might be scheming. She was reminded by me how I had spent many moons forgetting about people. Try not to cross your galleass 'cause you are going anyhow!

Changing times

Patches and mealy-mouth Ziggy got served up their connoisseur's breakfast; we took our seats in the saddle and were on our way to the homecoming. Well you never know who is to ride shotgun, give out order all the while and who will be the pulling on the reins.

I was sort of hoping it would be my turn to decide who had the opportunity of pointing the horses in the right direction. I am steering away from that some, so just let it be said that got decided it would be me, to get started off. I always minded "this and that" however that wasn't going to last long before being spelled. I have come to grips with never living it down of once scratching a fender. It seemed some fifty years of shore 'nough accident free practice suddenly lost any clout acquired in the matter. In as much as "stop the car and let me out" or turn loose of the reins are the only two acceptable alternatives offered is reason why I keep a large bottle of nerve pill in the car. Some people can do a number on the nerves more so than those of a black man sneaking in at the polling place on Election Day in Alabama.

While making our way back to the ancestral land we got dumped on with a heaping big rain squall, but that is a story for another time, When it became light enough to regain our bearings it appeared people from sea to shinning sea had a shot at being soaked to the gills. Thoughts got aroused and the granddaddy of them was would their parade get rained on and cancelled before it got underway. Recon one might say only a dampener was cast over the festivities as there were only tiny rain drops falling now and again when we tied up.

Any doubt as to who may have come was put to rest when we arrived and sized up the vehicles. They were all old folk's cars and narrow one had license for way over yonder folks. I like to have never made it on inside, but did momentarily until "eyes" ushered me back out. Me and the Misses stopped outside at the front door and jawed a spell with a man minding the donation bucket. Wanda thought we might help them a little to defray expenses, so she dropped in a few coins. I was thinking on being proud of her about that until I did go inside and take a gander at the financial sheet. These people are far more able to help defray my expenses than me theirs, so while I am proud of her attitude it did get my goat some.

In no way are my intensions to be critical or judgmental with thoughts on homecomings. The Lilbert Community Homecoming has slipped more than one notch or two since those early years of the 30's. I don't know, just may not ever go again. In those good old days dinner on the grounds was dinner on the ground. Bed sheet were sometime spread out to keep the piss-ants from nibbling away on the victuals. People mingled and sampled each others fried chicken, and if victuals showed up what they had not been eating a lot of the last month or two they could help themselves to that as well. It was a time when a few women folk tried to outdo each other with their sweet tater pies or who had made the best looking bonnet to wear. The church house would be jammed packed with people with as many outside doing their thing. Yep, "time changes everything" so it is said but I had just as soon offer resistance and hang on to old memories of homecoming of how it once was.

We are bombarded pretty much daily from all four coroners of the fast paced lifestyle the world has graced or encumbered itself with. I guess the desire to move on up to the East Side is responsible for making every moment account toward that. I got to thinking on the such likes and quickly realized this is one of them deep subjects which scatter out in a lot of directions. Knowing I only have a few more years to have a brain I just decided to park that too for a spell, probably even to when I take my leave, as my last New Year's resolve was to not get more irons in the fire and have to go away with much unfinished stuff.

As I was saying, to me we are like a fleet of small boats out in he sea floating in and out of port with all the tides. Older boats often times gets stuck in the mud while the newer one has the steam to even buck the tide if they so like. It is for certain all people will leave on a journey to a happier hunting ground or worse, never to show up again. How we let go of each other has shore took a different turn since bygone day. There are some stuff which has to be "knocked before trying" to have the opportunity of knocking it. Some people wants to get burned up and their ashes scattered oven "ten-buck-2" A "wing-ding" is launched where the partying is a big celebration of people "carrying on the such likes" are not so common place. A good time is had by all as they move into reality of being here today and gone tomorrow. No monuments with epitaphs are erected to commemorate a life which once was.

We here at Wandaland have just entered into a drought. It has been two days since it has rained in the month or so. According to my favorite Weather Prophet we just might be out of the woods here and about. Sort of hate to hear talk like that 'cause now

I got to pull the rope on the mowing machine. The darn thing has a mind of its own. A whack of two with laying a few "four letter words" on it will usually cause a backfire and puff of smoke after the lesson of just who is the machine and who is the operator.

Well folks that is how stuff has been here at Wandaland where the cows are always hungry, don't give up milk and fat-cat is sassy as ever. kp

MAKING MEMORIES

Here we go again with news from Wandaland about kissing, necked women and those darn grasshoppers while the cows are hungry and don't ever get milked.

It was a day or so ago when I received an email from a cousin which contained a cute cartoon of a two year old child having "the first kiss." This child was attempting to kiss something or someone through a glass window. I sort of believe my son Tim (Timothy Aaron) may have had his first kiss along about one year old with his dog Brownie. He and Brownie had a marvelously improved relationship. Brownie was a girl dog who had one set of puppies before getting "fixed". When Tim would be playing outside in the front yard Brownie would always stay between him and the street. Tim you may not recall, but you had two dogs which looked pretty much the same named Brownie. Your little friend Laurie Jean at Little Cypress loved your Brownie Dog as much as you so it seemed. The last Brownie didn't make it when we moved to Alaska.

I don't know, but just maybe my first kiss was with a mule or a cute little baby pig. I think I can remember a girl in the third grade of primer school trying to kiss me, but it never happened. Boys at that age aint to crazy about getting any girl germs. But we soon grow out of that! I did have a short lived "luv life" once when about 12 years young. Oh yes, I still remember the girl.

Sue Hill came to spend the summer with her cousin Anita which lived next to us at Oak Flat. I guess it could be said that Sue and I came to like each other right away. It seems if that was just the expected thing, and probably encouraged a little by different ones. That summer was filled with swimming with neighborhood kids, and having neighborhood parties at night. Summer that year ended too soon, and there was a day Sue would return to her home in California. I walked Sue back to her cousin's home while holding hands the night before leaving the next morning. I think we both knew we wanted to kiss, and it happen, well if rubbing closed lips together is kissing. I don't know about her, but I could just feel eyes trained on me as we hugged, perhaps knowing at least sub-consciously we would never see each other again, but we did promise to write.

I painted the boat daddy had built that year, after Sue had left, and printed her name on each side of the bow. Naturally I got a little "teasing" about that. Sue and I would write to each other occasionally the next year or so. About the only thing I remember now is she wrote about a religious experience she was enjoying. Well the letters quit coming and I am pretty sure she quit receiving letters from me. I have sometime wondered about Sue and whatever may have happened. I just know in my heart she has had a wonderful life because of being a smart sweet lovely little girl she was.

Into a person's life come many different relationships. Some relationships we cherish, and others perhaps we wish were only a bad dream. Kids are somewhat transparent and they have a much different criteria than adults with respect to being and having a friend.

Kids are quick to forgive and forget and don't hold grudges! Perhaps such conduct as this is just one of the many reason why Jesus said unless big folks become like little kids they aint going to make the cut.

My guess is there is someone whom your life has crossed path with, much time in the past, that you like to think about now and again. So many times we are in the memory making business and don't even realize it.

Went to see Medicine Woman the other day and got thumped on. I had picked up a couple pounds somewhere according to her scales but never got hollowed at fur it. She sort of talked like if I made it through the summer everything would be alright. Also went to the low vision doctor thinking I was going blind. He didn't do any of that "better one, better two" stuff. Instead he fitted me out with spectacles doing just reading stuff and watching crawlers on TV. I should be like new once I hoof it on down to the hearing doc and get several balls of wax extracted from the hearing parts. Not shore I want to be new like that again. However Wanda says all the time "Can't you turn that television down some." She claims sometimes I only hear what I want to hear. I hear tell where there is smoke there is fire. Guess that could be a little on the right side of shore-'nough. I should strain my ears more to hear stuff she mumbles on account one day she is liable to say something really important that I want be grabbing hold on it.

It seems like there are several e-mails talking about watermelon seeds being planted at the White House for watermelons to be served at state dinners, etc. Another e-mail which caught my eye was a Scam Warning to older folks. If someone comes to your house pretending to be checking on older people during the heat and ask you to take off clothes and hold you hand up while doing a shuffle, don't do it. It is a scam, and of course "you know who" she didn't know that then and felt foolish afterwards. Some people just like to see older white women necked. Course old Fred Sanford said they are the ugliest people he had ever seen. Ole Fred had other kinds of issues, seems like he was allergic to work and often told Elizabeth he was having "the big one,"

My innards has done started to growl and rumble again so I am thinking on going to look for a cold biscuit left over from the morning feeding to hush them up with.

Then I got to put out some feed (poison) for all those grasshoppers hopping around in the yard. I had just as soon let them be so I wouldn't have to mow so often. Anyway that was the last chore she put in the "job jar." So folks, recon it's time to hop to it and that is about how things have been here at Wandaland where the cows are always hungry and never get milked, kp

Reflections of Days Gone By

Some people seem to do their best reflecting on the past while sitting on "the throne." (I noticed a day or so ago mounted next to the toilet seat in a home was a magazine rack with a few "good house keeping magazines and homes and gardens in it) Just thought I would take a look to see if there was a Popular Mechanic, but there wasn't.) Howdy folks, this is Wandaland coming at you from way over here where the cows are always hungry and never gets milking.

Before the days of cell phones there were those who had made their "throng room" (powder room, rest room, the crapper, folks a Mr. Crapper invented the thing and that is why it is sometimes called a crapper, and that is for real) a telephone booth as well to do "jaw jacking" about present day stuff. I am talking light years ago when all telephones had a cord attached to them coming from inside the wall, on from poles and far away places.

Well, there is multi-tasking, and there is multi-tasking for different folks, don't ye know? The whole world, so it seems, has became one gigantic telephone booth. My six month saga of seeking out a place where there are no bars, not even the tiny ones you have to strain your eyes to see on Wamda's cell phone, is perhaps good news to "sing-u-lire" folks. I am in favor of restaurants posting signs at the front door "no shores, no shirts, and cell phones, no service." Wouldn't do any bellyaching if all them TVs disappeared either,

Back in the "good ole day", well so I am told, when ye rode "old Liz" into a civilized town you had to leave your "six shooter" at the Marshall's office, so why not cell phones? Just aint gone-uh happen, so you say! I don't think cell phone are allowed inside East Texas Medical Center for calling out, and I don't know if they will ring either, but any way here is Wanda's cell phone number: 1-214-543-0554, ETMC main number (Patient info and stuff) is 1-903-597-0351. Sorry, there is no 1-800 number, and they are so cheap, there is only single ply "wipes" in the public cr, uh, toilets.

Speaking about ETMC, tomorrow is the big day, and wow have to be there at 5:30 A.M. It is about 1-1/2 hr drive too, so the ole alarm will probable be set for at least 4 am and maybe a bit more.

I was given some peculiar kind of disinfection soap to scrub down with a time or two before coming in. Guess the last time I was in I must have smelled a bit raunchy.

I just may even "up them one", and go get a hair cut as well. Been getting quite a bit of mail from people, well all over from the US, up in Alaska, over in Ireland, and down under in New Zealand, making mention of praying for the doctor, his helpers, Wanda and me, and folks, I just want to say I appreciate it a lot. A dear friend sent me a poem about New Years, and reflecting on the past. Its main message is "friends" is what life is about. Judy, I don't think I ever said how much I enjoyed it and how appropriate it was for New Year's.

Well it is about time to wake up the Doctor's office and see if he is going to be there tomorrow cause if he is planning on being a "no show" so am I, and just think how unhappy that is gone-uh make some folks. I just hope he reserved the OR thing, ha. Guess I need to go now and see about the hair cut, so until next time this is Wandaland from over here where the cows are always hungry and never needs milking. kp

Renee's Salmon catch

Cherished Memories

Hello everybody from Wandaland where the cows are always hungry, never needs milking and where Patches the dog greets everyone with a friendly bark and wagging tail. There was this fairly wealthy fellow named Job in the Good Book, and it seems like he had terrible things come upon him which brought on excessive miseries which is sort of hard for us to understand. Anyway, he lost all his kids, horses and mules, cattle and other critters. Even his "significant other" accused him of having a breath which stunk like a sewer! As we read on we see where things got a whole lot better. What he had to say concerning all his losses was "the Lord gives and the Lord hath taken away."

I am wondering how often we apply that scripture to events which we bring on ourselves. Of certainty the Lord has a permissive will and allows many things of our own doings to come to pass No doubt about it as to the Lord has exclusive control over some things and He does give and take away things such as good and terrible weather. It is "hard" sometimes, even a stretch, to be "content in all things" which we know beyond a shadow of doubt are "the Lord's doings." I recon one of the main lessons to learn in the story of Job is to take inventory of our lives as to our motives for serving Him. Do we serve to receive blessings, or do we serve the Lord because of who He is and the blessings are just bonuses? It is my believe the devil can no longer go to the Lord and ask for us to be "considered" and have a "golden zap" come down on us even when our motives are bad. That is to be take care of later on!

The Lord gives us rainy cold Saturday mornings and it is up to us to "make the best of the day" without grumbling, and "bellyaching" or thinking God owes us an answer to the "whys" of life. Sure, our parades gets "rained on", and they were to be lovely parade too. Do we not sometime forget that God provides what is best for us instead of what we want? Is it not up to us to be excited about what God has in store for us each morning before we "roll out of bed", "hit the deck" running. We may have thought about "building Rome" on a particular (rainy cold Saturday) day, but we were given the opportunity to "sleep a little later, to just relax in bed and savor the second, maybe even the third cup of coffee, and just think about "stuff" until you "run out" of pleasant stuff to think about.

As we think on stuff and allow our minds to drift back to days separated by a lot of time we, come to realize many were days of making memories. We never though of "living" in those days as making memories to be recalled at a time when there wasn't much else left to do. There were moments of the past which caused the heart to pound so fast and hard you wonder if others could hear it. One was the time you saved a seat on the school bus for the boy you had hoped would sit beside you on the way home. As you watched him walk down the isle of the bus to where you were seated you quickly removed your books from the empty seat beside you as he approached. He stopped for a moment and just stared at the empty seat and asked if anyone was sitting there. All you could say was "do you see anyone?" It didn't seem like a silly question and answer at the time, especially to you. The next question which just seems to be one you placed in his mouth for him was if it was okay if he sat there. Not wanting to let it show you had been "dying" for him to ask, you simply said "that's your business."

Your head was "spinning" so when he sat down that you did not hear the jeers which came from the back of the bus. That was a moment you have treasured all these years. It was the start of a sure meaningful relationship to last during the time the black hair each had would be turning to silver and on in the "winter years" of life. There were to be many other moments in life cherished forever; memories which will never fade away or be crowded out of memory by "demands of the day."

What about the eighteenth birthday, the first birthday after being a married person? There was no money for a present, not even a small bracelet. The big bouquet of wild flower were prettier and appreciated more by you than if they were orchards. It said "I love you" in ways which could never be said in words. The "starter house" wasn't really much but in those days you saw it as a mansion. Much later in life dad takes a picture of a son in uniform from the table or shelf and look at it a moment recalling taking him for his first hair cut and wonder "where has all the time gone." Ah yes, memories which are born out of love are so private, cherished and lasting. Though we sometimes try recalling them in words can never express how they make us feel inside.

Today just happened to be one of those rainy cold Saturday morning, but "this is a day the Lord has made, and we're to be happy in it", so I think I'll give it my best shot. There isn't a lot of exciting news from Wandaland this week other than the good rain we have had. The shed for the "Flintstone Car" has been placed on hold for a while and I was hoping to work on it some today, but the Lord had other plans. Wanda is going to therapy two or three time a week for her shoulder and I "play around" with a few "workout machines" there while they are "babying" her, ha. The corporation she is manager of had its' annual meeting this week and I have been quite busy helping getting ready for it. My how "time flew by" as February is doggone near gone. It want be long now until we will go see Renee. (I had a dream last night of preparing to go there.) I have became aware of Sherry Abbott having a new e-mail address and also that Donna Reeves will be publishing a new letter very soon which will be primarily focused towards music. We wish her much success with it and I would imagine that many of you will want to be on her mailing list. I notice reading the ads in the Lake Area Leader where Hazel is back at Sue's Roost there in Eustace. It is where they have good chicken and dumplings on Wednesday nights. My latest magazine having the TV programs listing for RFD-TV came yesterday and there are some interesting ads in it as well. There is one where we can obtain a free detailed blueprint of Mammy's 1895 Chicken House. Wanda wants us to send for it. There is another one for Goat Worker advertising a pen which is supposed to allow for the ease of use and comfort of goat handling. We don't have any goats, well not yet. I have been sort of expecting some of the neighbors' to drift on down this way though. It is hard to imagine but I suppose that some of you do not know about RFD-TV which is Rural America's Most Important Network. Meredith Hodges also has an ad for her tapes on training Mules and Donkeys. Until next time that's 'bout it from Wandaland where the cows are always hungry, never needs milking and Patches stand guard at the driveway. Later . . . . kp

Big Doings at Wandaland

There is some big doings in the works for Wandaland where the cows are always hungry and never gets milking. We were ailing with the miseries some Thanksgiving day but had a nice quite dinner at home anyway. When Wanda turns to and puts her mind to it she makes me proud every time with the vittles. While we were out and about messing around with the city folks one of those bugs crawled off one of them on to us and we were nigh house ridden for a few day. I called our Medicine Woman to see if she would make a house call and got laughed at. I just might stop helping her pay for that Volkswagen she drives.

Recon this week I will dig through the receipt box to find cooking on fancy vittles to carry to Nacogdoches for the Parker Christmas Party Reunion Extravaganza. I have never cared for sweet taters since those depression days when we had a bumper crop. There were so many taters they were also fed to the hogs to fatten them. Folks there are hundreds, maybe even thousand of way to cook those roots. They weren't to bad eating raw, except if you ate a bait of them you would come down with the belly ache. We had that musical fruit fried, boiled, baked, and stewed. You could even make desert and soup with them. What I had in mind to say was not so long ago I got introduced to a sweet tater casserole and I actually liked it. It was yummy, yummy. Well, I hope some one else will have such a craving for it too on account of I am going to try my luck with it for the partying. Then I got to scat on down to Tractor Supply and walk out with some kind of man gift to take along. This time I am going to leave Wanda behind when going to Tractor Supply Store. Last time I let her loose in there I could not drag her out for looking at all the stuff folks like us can use out here Wandaland.

This year I am going to try and beat Jolene mailing out Christmas Cards, but I probably won't make it. By the way, she makes some of the best candy and brings it each year to the party, and there are some of you who really don't know what you are missing. Then Christmas Time is already on its way, and I hear there was a big run on department stores last Friday by people getting in some early shopping. One of these days I might just do that again myself just for the heck of it. I guess it just would not be Christmas without such things as this and anticipation of the day and our favorite music. I suppose mine is "O' Holly Night and "Winter Wonder Land." My daughter,

Teresa Ann sees to it that a stocking is hung for us for Santa to fill with "goodies" for me and the little woman.

Well we will no sooner turn around twice putting all the pretty ribbons away from the gift and it will be time to sit back in the easy chair and watch the folk in the Big Apple see the ball drop marking a new year where many New Years Resolutions comes into effect. I don't do that any more that is make resolutions on account of I can't think of any new ones and the old ones didn't work "nohow."

Had some exciting news a day or so ago as youngest daughter is in the process of making me grandpa in May of 2009 year This will be her first and I guess she was afraid the biological clock was about run down. No, she is not that old, just probably got all of her big trips over with and became intrigued with the Doctor Spock manual. There was a sonogram but no determination if the baby will be a sitter or pointer.

Alan & Diane NZ Cousins

Another bit of exciting news is Wanda's cousins in NZ are planning to visit us along about September of next year (in 2009). We received a pretty calendar from them as well and I am not sure if I let that be known, so thanks Diane a whole bunch. It is a bit windy today, actually gusting, which reminds me of the wind blowing across the prairie in the Dakotas. I'm thinking a sentimental journey to renew some old acquaintances in those parts and it should be put on the "to do list."

Recon that is the way it is here at Wandaland where the cows are always hungry and never get milked. Wanda and I are looking forward to seeing the clan in Nacogdoches directly. Until next time let your engine idle a bit now and again. kp

Traditions

Here it is five-thirty in the morning and I am up, wide awake and have already had a couple mugs of coffee. Howdy all, this here is Wandaland coming at you from way over here with a bit of "this and that" where the cows are always hungry and never need milking.

Rudolph, the most famous Reindeer of all has made his rounds and put out to pasture "out there" in Santa Land. Yep, Christmas for 2006 is history, well sort of. Tiny tots are playing with new toys, school is in long recess with school boys kicking footballs around in the yard, moms and dads are carrying arm loads of awful looking clothes back to trade. Even this Ole Santa made out with a lot of loot this year. I do want to thank everyone who did not give me underwear this year as there is a package or two in the dresser drawer getting bathed in "good smelling stuff." Speaking of that, I want to thank everyone for not giving me "Old Spice" this year too, as I still have a good ten year supply. I did "make out" like "gang busters" though as Wanda gave me a Claddah Ring to replace the one I lost, which she got for me when in Ireland in 2004. Ah yes, maybe we put Ireland back on the sightseeing list again, but our hopes after Disney in Florida is New Zealand.

Wanda NZ vacation 2008

Wanda and I made a long annual pilgrimage to be with daughter and family of many kids and grandkids, the Saturday before Christmas and did the same Christmas Day (after Wanda got her beauty sleep over with, as if she need it) to well chartered places to visit other family members which we do for a Christmas Dinner celebration. It was a real joy to see tiny tots empty their stocking and tare the wrapping from pretty packages as if though they didn't much care they were wrapped in pretty bright colored paper at all.

With various New Year's Parties taking place as well as going to Grandma's house for Christmas, I got to thinking on "traditions." I had a fellow employee in Alaska which seems to have thought if there was once a New Year's party it constituted a tradition. I did not think so, even though I was not against having or commencing a tradition of such, ha. Guess I liked to kiss all the pretty girls (but only back then Wanda) as the clock struck in the New Year as well as anyone else. As we were, back to traditions.

One day my curiosity got the best of me to consult someone who knows about this stuff, so I went to the encyclopedia to get me some old fashion "book learning" on the matter. Now the word tradition is not one of those two city block long college word you get sprung on you causing a reaction like someone who has just arrived in town on a turnip truck. Recon this isn't the only little word I have been ignorant of its real meaning of more than three scores and ten years or so. I had a good enough understanding of words to get by on I guess. Anyway, I and all my rowdy friends never had a problem of knowing what we meant when conversing. Sometimes we hear people use certain words which impress us, sounds good and stuff and we want to use them too, even though like the gal says on TV "I totally don't know what that means."

According to the encyclopedia which I do "totally rely on" every now and again, tradition in "American" (English) is from a Latin word which means "to hand down" or "hand over." (From all I know it was early Grecian people who spoke a language in the region Latium who had their language imported to other civilizations or cultures, and that is how the word "Latin" came into being. We are told that Latin is a dead language, but we still keep on using it a lot, go figure?) Words down through the years have a way of becoming something than what they once did. For instance gay, well I want go any further with that as I am sure y'all "catch my drift." Well, here in this country we are much prone to use "hyperboles" and allow the context of conversation to let it be known what is meant. Should I to say "he has a belly full of that" and while it is highly probable an overstatement, we need to know just what the "that" is to truly understand. (Often times a little body language helps get a message over too.)

Tradition here in America, and probably other places as well, has came to mean "something" such as a practice being handed down from one generation to another. (People up at the North Pole probably don't have traditions as they are plenty busy just trying to stay warm.) Traditions can be an individual act repeated on various occasions.

It is sometime said certain "things" or "happenings" in a church are traditions. It is a tradition to send Christmas Greeting Cards and birth announcements. It was a tradition to give to our kids stuff they really like, such as a hugh jar of olives to one, and cherries to another, and sometime that still happens just for "old time sake."

It could very well be a tradition to have a New Year's Celebration, such as a party, or even a Church Prayer Service It may be a tradition for a church or school to have a "teen age lock in" on Halloween night. It has become a tradition for many people to make "New Year Resolutions" and of course to "fall off the wagon" too.

As I was thinking on "traditions", a simile came to mind, well sort of. A tradition could be similar to an expensive fine set of China Ware a lady proudly keeps displayed in her China Cabinet which is used only on very special occasions. It is used only once a year perhaps on her marriage aniversity. As it was once being taken out and placed on the dinning table a cup was dropped getting its handle broken off. There was a "frightful kind" of despair which came over the lady with a little wringing of hands as well. Her romantic candle light dinner went on as planned, but in her mind she could see the broken cup once in a while. Little did she realize the broken cup set into motion actions later on where there would have to be dreadful decisions. She thought about sending the cup out and having the handle, which was still in one piece, refastenrf. She also though about other things as the cup was placed back in the China Cabinet where the broken handle would not show. The cup handle was carefully placed inside the cup. Time continue to go on, month after month until the month of her aniversity came once again. She remembered about the broken cup handle.

Her thoughts were to skip the candle light aniversity dinner this year and just pretend it was forgotten. After all there were a number of other important things which she needed to devote attention to. So after five years it was skipped that year. It was much easier the following year to omit the romantic candle dinner. And so it was, a tradition which had much meaning had an interruption with the possibility of being lost to a regrettable memory.

The lady wanted to commence using the fine china as if it were not something special. No! no! NO! Please don't do that. Tell the lady traditions are "memory maker" and they are a bit like promises made. They can usually be kept or explained and reasoned away. I suppose except for things related to God, the only thing which does not change is change. From "time to time" some things which are important to us have a way of changing to being lesser important. And there are a number of things which should occupy a place of high importance in life which should never change. It is not terrible hard to sort out what is important in life and what isn't. It is often times very difficult to "put off", that is to say not attend to, pressing matters to attend to the more important matters. "Things" don't usually just happen; they have to be made to happen. More likely than not, if something is important to us it will get accomplished one way or another. What a sad thing it would be to reach the winter years of life and mostly all a person has in the way of memories are a lot of

"I whish I had." Then again, the most wonderful thing is to exit the winter years with your house in order.

Happy New Year to all, from Wanda and me, here at Wandaland where the cows are always hungry and never needs milking; where Old Patches thinks his calling in life is to chase Ziggy and eagerly beg for a "hand-out." It will probably be "sometime" before the airwaves will be bringing New again, so that is how it is for now. kp

THE BIG CLAN GATHERING

Hey Lougal, this is Wandaland knocking.

As many anticipate the announcement concerning the first Saturday in December hearts will be aglow with Thanksgiving and perhaps enjoying Christmas music. Some favorites of many are Silver Bells, Dreaming of a white Christmas and Santa Clause is coming to town. I am quite certain the one I love the very best is "Holey Night. My first time to hear it was when John Walton of "Walton' Mountain" was coming home late in a terrible snow storm Christmas Eve and stopped in a Black Church while their Christmas program was ongoing to thaw out a bit. Only a handful of people were there and needles to say John was welcomed in. The black minister led the few people attending in Oh Holy night. I suppose, well in my diminishing mind, there has never been a television program series to equal "Walton's Mountain."

I am asking you to please forward this note to all relative in your address book as I want to urge upon everyone to attend that possible can. Yes I know there are many who lives in far away places in other states and there is yet time to make plans and preparation to attend. Just why I do not know but I feel as if there will be many attending this year.

In the mdst of much heartache and grief since the beginning of the year many had the occasion to see others they haven't seen since the days of their youth but what a wonderful privilege it is to gather together in a different circumstance.

It was a few years prior to 1977 that a few family came together probably more so as a "reunion" as well as a Christmas Party. It was not uncommon for some families to spend the night of Christmas Eve playing card games before and after 1977, near these entire pioneering relative" which started this tradition have already completed "life's Journey" here on earth. It is feasible to believe they are watching us from heaven and even we can feel their presence though no longer with us.

Now I want to mention each year it becomes a sacrifice for someone to attend and because this event happens on the same day of the year it has preeminence on their calendar of significant events for this special month of the year and the sacrifice even becomes more meaningful to them.

This I want to say to you who are a few generations after me. This event was chose to occur each year as a day of non interference to each others observance of their immediate family celebrations. By reason of longevity this tradition has been handed to you to enjoy and keep alive. To those not familiar it is not like a reunion I attended (not in this family of relative) where you had to show proof of being dipped for fleas and ticks before gaining entrance. Feel no need to bring a biscuit in a brown bag because there is always much traditional food as if it were a "barn rising."

So "y'all come" even if the law is out hunting you down for things like cattle rustling or horse stealing as you will have no reason to feel "out of place."

Before closing I like to say a few chosen words to my children, grandchildren and great grandchildren. As I stand in front of the mirror after scrubbing off body part dirt for my weekly bath and shaving, I look in the mirror and think how lucky "me squeeze" is to have been able to take papers out on such a handsome, romantic dude such as I.

Another message I trust you "grown-up curtain climbers'" will take as serious is this. The little cabinet where I often reminded to put back the shaving cream, old spice, and other "foo-foo" stuff in preparation for "happy hour", yeah that is right "hour" will hold no more of this stuff as it is a good five year supply.

Now I get to share a couple drawers of the twelve drawer dresser with my squeeze wherein there is no more room to stuff more long handles, boxer shorts, tee shirts and all those beautiful unmatched socks. May I make a suggestion what to send me for Christmas? Each of you Just think if each of you would send greenbacks of $100.00 there would no more cause for me to be playing the "one arm bandit" each week because my dream of becoming a millionaire would come true. Course some how or another all "ill legit" descendents would have to chip in as well.

Louse, please do not include Wanda if you do send this out to one and all on account I want to be around to see everyone in a few days.

Love, best wishes, happy Thanksgiving, and all that stuff from you highly esteemed uncle Kodell who is head wrangler here at Wandaland where the cows are always hungry and we don't milk-em. kp

Thanksgiving Day

Greeting from Wandaland where the cows are always hungry, seldom ever get milking, and where the big new on the front page of our weekly is who won the football game, and what dude crossed the finish line the most with the ball. It has been a bit cool here of late. You have a lighter side of new this week from over here and abouts.

In just a few days all of America will be celebrating Thanksgiving, each perhaps in their own way. Some may go to a football game and have a tailgate turkey leg while fellowshipping with friends and waiting for stadium doors to open. There will be a lot of others who will spend the day with relative, grandmas and grandpas, enjoy a traditional meal with all the family seated around the table where someone will voice a Thanksgiving Prayer for the clan. Perhaps mid evening some pumpkin pie and a cup of coffee will be enjoyed as one of the parades are watched on the tube. There will also be much sadness in the lives of some people as they learn of recent loss of family members or relatives.

I like the stories we learn in the second grade in school of how "thanksgiving day" commenced. Maybe some of it is not true, but it does not matter so much as I can still believe in what it means to me, just more than the traditional ways of observing it, and I do not see much, if anything wrong with that. America the beautiful, from sea to shinning sea, America, home of the free and brave. America, the champion of freedom.

We do not have church sponsored religion where there is a "tithe" collected once a year to support it. We are free to worship or not worship according to the dictates of our own hearts. May our prayer song always be "God Bless America, land that I love" and our "sweet liberty." May it always be printed on our monies "In God We Trust." There is probably no person, child or adult, male or female, in any country which can not point to our "Old Glory" and say that is the flag of that great country, the United States of America.

When the "color guard" passes the "colors" in review, I can not but help having a feeling come over me which makes me proud of being so blessed to live in this country. I have a faster heart beat, and here of late have to fight against tears.

I am proud to live in a country where our "armed forces" consists of volunteers. Where young women and men feel it is their duty, and give them selves without reservation to insure individual and corporate freedom and liberty.

A good many years ago Dr. Albert Einstein gave a speech which has become very famous, and should represent the "fabric" of every American. In substance he said "every day I realize how earnest I must apply myself just to give back to society a small amount of what society has given to me." You may have heard the commercial of one of the chemical companies which salutes the American farmer. In it they recognize all of our wellbeing and happiness depends upon the American farmer. How many times a day do we take a drink of water and never give it one thought if it is safe. Our wellbeing is much dependent upon others, such as volunteer services from fire departments and at hospitals. Baxter Black, from "out there" sits in his rocking chair late evening when the shadows are growing long and make some good observations. He takes "note" how quite and peaceful it is there on his front porch, noticing the clouds silver linings, and hearing his "woman" putting together some "grub" while he sort of sits and mediates on "things." His conclusion about life is: he is one of luckiest people in the entire world to be born in America, and that it "just doesn't get any better than this." But he doesn't really contribute it all to luck either, because he recognize if was not for service men and women now, in the past, and future just where would he be?

Most everyone will have opportunity to "rub elbows" with a military person of our armed forces in uniform the next few days as Thanksgiving: approaches. Please consider speaking to them and say "Sir or Miss Thank you for being in the service." Say it with meaning, and if it appears you will not have such an opportunity, and then make the opportunity. Quite often opportunity will not present itself. "Just Do It." I can "guarantee" you will feel "real good" all inside for doing it, and so will the serviceperson.

Well folk, drive safely, have a nice holiday, and Wanda and I are looking forward to seeing all of you at "the party" which is approaching must too fast. And that is about how it has been here at Wandaland where the cows are always hungry and never gets milked since last writing y'all. Kp

Self Improvement

Most mornings when I "fire-up" the computer there is an e-mail, which apparently has wide circulation, sent out by a lady named Gail. I look forward to them immensely as they are always so positively "uplifting" and motivating with "thoughts" of Ralph Marston. For all you guys and dolls who wear Wranglers you probably would call it "cowboy wisdom." It really does set in motion the "small amount" of mind I have left thinking about self-improvement stuff! (I can no longer afford to give people a "piece of my mind, as I have so little left, ha.) "Self improvement" should concern most people, and who is it that could not use a little self-improvement once in a while? Take me for instance when I think I am "right about everything", as I am accused of sometimes. People who think they are "right" all of the time set them selves up to "no learning." And those who are a bit dogmatic in winning an argument usually win more than the argument; they win resentment of the other person. I suppose one of the things which place humans "above" animals is our ability to consider others' "point of view" and just agree to not agree, keeping respect for the other person

There are things which seem to annoy me at times, being just a little short of really getting on my nerves and driving me crazy. (Just bet you have those kinds of experiences as well.) As for me, I do not like so much to hear clocks going "tic-tock" on and on and on. I know, some people love to hear such as it is a soothing sound to them as water trickling over bed rock down a creek. Clocks are time machines cranking off time, seconds by second. With each "tic-tock" a couple seconds slips out into the atmosphere to go on to eternity past and never return again. If somehow there could be a "time line" stretching out of eternity past into eternity furture, just imagine what we could fit on it. Imagine the line is made up of segments of centuries. Inside the centuries we could fit decades, then in decades years and into years, months, weeks, days, hours and so forth. Time is said to be "marching on", and we can't harness or control time. The best we can do is to invent devices to sort of fool ourselves about time. We invent all kinds of "new beginning" with time, such as a new hour, a new day, a new week, a new month and a new year. We do it with clocks and calendars. It appears to me Mr. Webster had a hard time defining "time" and I am not sure he got it right.

Perhaps of all things ever said about time there is one we don't pay a whole lot of attention to: "Sixty seconds makes a minute, how much good can I do in it. Sixty minutes makes an hour, I'll do the best that's within my power. Twenty-four hours makes a day, "time" for work, rest and play." And the time machines keep on cranking off "tic-tocks." The Holy Bible seems to indicate we humans should keep track of our sojourn on planet earth in terms of days rather than years, and I have an idea why we don't. Not long ago I asked a lady how old she was. Her reply was "not old enough for medi-care, or for old fools to be caring." (I think she thought it was none of my business and took the opportunity to fib a bit as well!)

I'm still "pondering over" (multi-tasking) why I didn't get a lot of sleep a night or so ago. Was it because my left nostril was not taking in air and needed lubricating, and because there was a place on my back that needed scratching badly which I couldn't reach? Some nasal sprays now come in pump bottles which has a "shaft" to stick up your nose long enough to reach the sinus cavity. It took a little "doing" (pumping) to get the pump to pumping and the nostril un-clogged.

As to scratching of the back I had to hop out of bed and find a door opening to rub my back on. I nudged Wanda a time or two and asked her to scratch it for me but she being half asleep politely mumbled that wasn't on the "PNA" (pre nuptial agreement). I had actually thought that it was, and we had agreed to scratch each others' backs on an as needed basis. It was my good preacher friend who put me on to all the PNA stuff us older recycled "love sick" people aught to give concern to before being taken off the market once again. There should to be a meeting of the minds about things like "which side of the bed we get to sleep on, the kind of cereal for breakfast, the kind of laxative to take, who gets to handle the TV remote, and things like backs scratching, etc.

It was around two-thirty in the morning; just about the time the bottom fell out of the sky when the "no sleeping syndrome" commenced creeping up on me. It commenced to rain down "bull frog and tadpoles" as they seemed to be falling out of the sky for a while. The rain seems to have had an effect on my body's "holding tank" like a pot of coffee trying to fins its way out after taking those little tablets what makes a person pee.

My oatmeal boiled over yesterday morning, and I am talking like it made a big mess this time. It appeared the biggest majority of it creped out of the bowl, down the outside and sort of piled around the base of the bowl. Had it been dark it might resembled a volcanic eruption. I was so sure I had mastered the art of cooking oatmeal in the microwave that I turned my back on it while it was cooking. The catastrophe was so devastating it allowed the toast to burn and the entire situation delayed breakfast five minutes or so. A reconstruction of events did seem to indicate that none precise measurement of the heated water was the cause for the eruption and clean-up effort. Just a milliliter of water one way or the other seems to make a difference.

Self Improvement

The roof is now on the shed for the "Flintstone Car" but it lacks having the flashing installed where it ties into an existing building. Most likely installing the sides will be the next phase, and the flashing will get installed when the "mood strikes me" on that. I think Fred and Wilma would be proud of its home. Once it has a place to sleep then I will start to remodel it a bit, like make the carrying deck a little larger and installing means to pull a small trailer behind it.

Estleen, the sister who lives down in Nacogdoches County, said that Dorothy who lives just outside Tyler came by and collected her and Verna and they all went down to see Retha down in Beaumont. She was proud to report that Retha had lost a lot of weight and had a good recollection of people and events. She was wondering just when and where Wanda's shoulder surgery would be. It is scheduled for 7:30 A.M., February 2nd at ETMC Athens.

The coordinator talked like the surgery is no big deal, but it is the therapy afterwards that's a drag. The non use of the arm will be a hassle and she will require a little help with the "bolder holders" and other under-garments, socks, etc.

And that is how it is here at Wandaland where the cows are always hungry and don't ever get milked, or nothing so "clamming up." kp

ON RUNNING THE MOUTH

It is not an unusual thing for someone to be involved in writing instructions to others whom they do not know. Many places of employment encourage "avoiding oral instruction" for a number of worthwhile reasons. Depending on what the instructions concerns it could be prudent to dot most of the i's and cross all t's. Once again depending on the subject matter the instructor could be as nervous over the written instructions as coed virgins at their first spring break.

There is perhaps a number of ways to think about communicating be it oral, written or even in body language. Not a lot folks I rub elbows with seem to say or write just the right amount. I usually think to little is said or a lot more "BS" than you care to weigh in on with no boots. People who talk and talk and talk (write and write and write) are sometime accused of being a "motor mouth" or spouting away with a dose of mouth diarrhea. Some folks are not too delighted on having been sharing others unfortunate affliction. Those who say little may be accused of not wanting to make an 'ash' of them selves by exposing their ignorance.

Would not this be a dull journey if all world sojourners act and reacted the same in ways of communicating? I sort of enjoyed Clyde and Leonardo's discussion on reinventing the wheel, lightening, running water and other important things. Well you may have someone in mind, such as I, if asked to give you the time of day you first have to listen how the stuff insides makes the time piece tick. I guess sometimes it is just best to excuse your self and leave the person in their own space talking to the wind.

Fragments of thoughts stored in brain cells have a way of coming together faster than old Ziegler (Ma's Pussy Cat) can find a new piece of real estate to unearth for a deposit. Sometimes alley cats scoot out faster than a dose of salts going through a widow woman. I'm not "fixing" to get strung out on something else, but hang with me bit. Nat King Cole sang a song about falling in love.

The thought has serviced (SURFACED) a couple time if I should ever "fall out of love" with my Apple Dumpling, my hunk, my squeeze, my sugar in the morning, sugar in the evening and sugar at super time, I would probably regroup, get a grip on the "rebound" and set my sights on another. And so, just who that might be? I had considered my Lady Medical Doctor but she has left me in the lurch. Poor woman went to Wisconsin. I am wondering if she likes cheese all that much. There are certain people who think I had a crush on her already. (Sorry no mentioning of a name allowed) So how does this affect the cost of a six pack? I don't know but she listens real well, and her "talking" made (since-sense & cents). She could persuade a monkey to stop making all those facial expressions or trying to "make love" to a football.

Why, just one day while sitting on the examining bench as she flipped pages of records, naturally informing me of too much weight gain, probably looking to see where she should commence the "thumping" her talking gained speed. After one or two uh-hu's she probably noticed me showing body language of nerve hormones being activated. She gave them a little boost with mumbling something about getting wormed. I see there is no record of you having a "finger wave" in more than a year she said. Right about then the anxiety attack gained a major foothold. You know Medi-care requires it for old men she said. OK, so what?

Well is seems like the "so what" was automatic deduction for Medi-care from my social security check might just stop and I would be hung out on a limb. See, I told you she knew how to get down to the not so nitty gritty in the gist of a matter.

I was then informed that I could be out-sourced for the "wave" or it could be an inside job. The benefits of an inside job were explained real well. So I hopped down off the table, dropped outer and underwear and started mooning.

She had pointed a long skinny finger at me and said you will have the benefit of a smaller finger, and it will be over and done with before dancing twice. There must be a point in relating this experience but at the moment I totally don't know why.

Somewhere along the journey of life my engine side tracked me for an overhaul on effective communicating. Atlanta is not a bad place to be side tracked for a while if you are young and single. It is also a big plus if there is an expense account where the terminator couldn't give a fig about "little incidentals." What Georgia says about their "Peaches" has a lot more to say before reaching the bragging stage. Course when people are young and single not a lot of crap in seminaries, where there are ripe Gorgeous Georgia Peaches, will sticks on the wall of memory. I am here to proclaim there are exceptions to many things. Not all horse-puckey slung against a brick wall will stick

So, why do some people engaged in "jaw jacking" 24/7, even with cell phones, in restaurants, in the John on the crapper, and at the breakfast table? That reminds me of a story I heard a long time ago and I just know you are at wits-end to hear it. There was this teenager (boy) who had not spoken a word in the last five years or so. This is not necessarily an unusual thing for modern day teens so I am told. One morning he came and took his place at the breakfast table and looked the situation over.

After "grace" he raised his head and "yelled out" "ah ship!" Naturally this astonished his parents who replied with "is something wrong?" He said "the biscuits are burned." That statement brought on a kind of panic from parents with the question "sons if you have been able to talk all these years, why haven't you?" His reply was "up to now everything has been alright!" Guess that could be an example of talking only when there seems to be a reason.

Like Mama Thelma Harper told her son Vinton in one of the re-runs, the big difference between horse manure and breaking wind is that horse manure serves more than one purpose. (Well that is the way I understood what was said.)

There probably is not a good definition of "effective communications" which fits all shoes. Someone has said it has taken place when a mental image has been planted and received from one mind to another. I don't know, perhaps so, speaking on effective. I have to admit a mental image is received when I get one of "those looks" from you know who, and it is usually effective. Who else could the "look" be from other than a pretty red hair gal who has red roots?

Mental images are no doubt being received and rejected when the "perfect ten" waltzing along swinging her hips in a teeny weenie poker dot bikini to the tune of "what's up Jack."

A reasonable guess as to why a lot of people 'talk' would be to relieve tension. Or it might just seem like the thing to do at the time under the present circumstances. A pleasurable or disgusting thing to us often times generates much dialogue.

Most of the time, well we like to think, not all talk is "idle talk" having no specific purpose other than talking. Much communications could probably be considered as a form of mind persuasion or mind control and it make little difference how it "comes at ye."

I guess a lot of people are a bit skeptical concerning their part of a conversation and look for "feedback" to determine if a full landing or just barely a stronghold has been made. We say things as "do you understand, do you see where I am coming from, have you considered my point of view?" People may say "work with me and hear me out" when a strong resistance is encountered.

It is no big revelation most people like to think they are at least moderately successful with planting a mental image and receiving feedback on how it is received. There is an old saying about fighting a fire with fire. Also, if you make a fist of the hand and shake it at someone, watch out for the feedback as it just might "floor you" in a home improvement project of having a few body parts rearranged.

To be understood as a compliment to all women of the universe, many are blessed with the gift of typing and gabbing at the same time. I once had a clerk who could smoke a key board generating seventy words a minute and at the same time carry on a reasonable sensible conversation with talk gusting up to the same intensity. OK Vern, aint that something!

There is ignorance and there is ignorance and then there is me. This is not like the fifteen year old daughter bouncing down stairs taking a seat at the breakfast table and saying Mom, Dad, I have something to tell you. She is asked what is it honey. The daughter isn't exactly the dimmest light bulb in the room and has plenty of experience to spare when it comes to soften up a blow. Just wanted to let you know I have become a woman! Dad took a quick glance at her hooters and says OK, is not like we have not noticed. Well there is a little more to it. I think I am a little pregnant. That little bombshell of speaking was a real "go get her" a wide awake attention getter to Mom and Dad. Dad's coffee commenced to taste like dishwater; knowing in such matters there is no such thing as a little. Perhaps there is "room" for a maybe, so you commence to ponder the odds. Sort of reluctantly dad asks how long she had been PG. Her reply was "since about 10 o'clock last night."

Once I went off up to Alaska to seek fame and fortune. Guess some things are never meant to be. After getting settled down and disposing of numerous "honey do" jobs in the job jar, I was faced with a lot of do nothing time. So the mind was put to ponder on what to do with an idle mind.

Getting a second employment was definitely ruled out as I was already paying too much income tax. I gave a little consideration of joining up with a political party but there was none who thought I had the "right stuff." So what do you after you scrape the bottom of the barrel racking the brain for something to relieve the stress of having too much time on your hand? You go to the university and get enrolled in courses as a career student hopefully getting a GED some day. Well like I said, sometimes things just don't jive. After about three semesters it came to me tests given would never be the same from one semester to the next. I have to tell you I have never looked on this as a failure. I want go into just why but the bottom line is everything learned will be used some way or another, hopefully before it becomes unlearned. That book learning was a big learning experience for me. Topping the list was becoming truly aware of how close to the edge of being totally ignorant I was and am. The more I went for book learning, the dumber I became. An English Professor said a lot of stuff I had already given thought to, and a new wrinkly or two was also introduced.

Book learning is the catalyst for a finished product often modulating life experiences. It was this professor, or was it Flip Wilson, who said not a lot of folks give a fig on how much you know, until it is known how much you care.

Among the few acquaintances I have there is an appreciation for each of them even though with one it is usually a struggle for me. This person can not do a lot of taking without me thinking about having the last words by saying "just go to hell." Don't recon many folks about like to find them selves in deep ship. Yeah, that is no misspelling! Lot of crap you have to just roll off the shoulder and it is always a good idea to allow people to "save face" There is this one person who seldom fails to pretend annoyed when I butcher the King' English. It would not be uncommon to be interrupted in speaking and be given a mini lesson on conjugation verbs. I never got the hang of that in the 7th grade, and I just like to have fun by messing with their head.

It won't be long before June 19th time or when my next "fingered wave" rolls around. Think I will opt to get "sourced out" next time since Dr Mary went crazy and has vamoosed to Wisconsin.

With this last little tidbit of observations it will be a wrap up. If you can "mess" with someone's mind without them getting wise to you, well you might be surprised what develops People who believes they have a card packing right to correct you, let it rip; you might even give them something which sticks out like a sore thumb. A couple light years ago I worked at "this place" with a couple dudes who were sharper than aged rat holes cheddar cheese. If something was being "worked on" and one was asked "how do you do a certain thing", if it wasn't like they were in hot pursuit of some personal comfort in the throne room, you could expect "let me show you."

There is nothing like keeping "it" simple and easy to understand. I went and looked up the word ten in a dictionary to see how it might be defined. It seems like Mr. Webster had people like me in mind when he wrote "a number which comes after 9 and before 11. I was sort of wishing for some long drawn-out definition that might give a Jet Engine Design Engineer something to put their teeth into.

Recon I had better saddle up and get on back to Wandaland where the cows are always hungry and never give any milk. Otherwise I might break a promise and get a little potty mouth or start teaching little kids some new four letter word. Until next time "give the world a smile every day" helping others along the trail. kp

Don't argue with Idiots

Dear friends and kinfolk, you have mail from Wandaland where the cows are always hungry, they never get milked and where we have resumed drinking regular tea.

As I was saying, there is not much (actually nothing) original with me. Dang it, I get scooped all the time with "old hat" stuff. All of the most important stuff in life I learned in primer grade school. I think up stuff, and low and behold I read where someone else "done" thought about the "such likes", seen, read or heard about it. I wish it was my original thought about something I have just read. "Never argue with an Idiot—they will drag you down to their level." (That could have come from a Democrat's opinion of a Republican or maybe the other way around.)

Here is one which applies to both side of the isle: "Congressmen who willfully take actions during wartime that damage moral and undermine the military are saboteurs and should be arrested, exiled or hanged!!!" President Lincoln the (Independent) President said that.

I listened a spell to a "spin doctor" who perhaps believes in stuff like we landed people on the moon first which gives us squatter rights, and he places credence in the Deviancy Code. Sarah's speech was supposedly full of code phrases. I wonder if that person was referring to "God bless America" as if only Republicans think of them selves as Americans. Get it? "God bless the Republicans." There is Hot Lips and Sweet Thighs I allow to have an audience once a twice a week. That is bending my ear on the tube, but I am blessed in that I won't ever have to meet any of these people in person. Maybe it is they who are the blessed ones. I got them "sized down & up", they are plumb stupid but probably owns a Condo or two and several Lexis automobiles.

It order to be have a balanced diet (uh in rhetoric) I been listening to some of Mr.B.O.' words as well and was surprised to learn he was either a "civil liberty" or "civil rights" lawyer before he embarked on "change" promoting a different career. But the dude I am fascinated the most with is a "flake" who calls himself a file. He is another person who should do some retracting before hand instead of afterwards. Guess he is waiting to see who spends their way into the "big house" before cooling down a bit. He is the same dude who brought it to the attention that Mr. McCain has four houses (which most likely belongs to wife Cindy). He then supposedly found out it is six instead of 4, and he pushed it up to six, and a day later nine. Maybe next week it will be twelve. (Mr. File just doesn't get it. He gets obsessed with negativisms and not able to let go of stuff, horse plucky stuff that is.

I had a fellow employee who came to work in Alaska with me. He was much enterprising, yet honest and hard working. He started off buying a 4-plex and kept investing until he had about twenty. I went by to visit with him the last time we went to Alaska. Although he is at least a millionaire now, he is still the same ole guy I fished with.

Who is it that has not seen a Perry Mason movie where each side attempts to introduce material which is ruled inadmissible? It is a deliberate act to place suspicions in the minds of a jury even thought inadmissible. A CNN robot (anchor) did just that thing yesterday. He just had to tell about some alleged misconduct of Sarah.

In the end the anchors also placed suspicions on what he had said and get this. He commenced his "spin" with his network had not confirmed the story, as if such can only be true if they confirmed it. Starting off this way is upfront weaseling. That is to plant "hearsay" storied. However the upfront disclaimer is supposedly ethical journalism.

There are often average batters in a game who faces a strong pitcher. The pitcher is very good at throwing curves making them look as if the batters had better step out of the box or else suffer a blow. Then there are experienced batters of courage who recognizes a curve ball from the moment it leaves the hand of the pitcher. Babe Ruth was a player who "struck out a number of times" but he hit home runs when it counted so his team could carry the pennant back home. Sarah and John hit the ball out of the park with their speeches, and they have the right stuff to keep doing in over and over. And there was Roger who could through a "hail Marry pass' when it was needed for the team to be a "Super Bowl" winner.

There is sad new today, and I don't fancy talking with you about such. I learned last night from my youngest sister (who is older than me) a lady went to meet her Lord and Savior a day or so ago. She was my Sunday School Teacher when I was just a lad at Oak Flat. Mrs. Inez Sitton was near 102 years old and enjoyed many good "bonus days" while sojourning here on earth.

Have a wonderful week-end, and to borrow a phrase from someone I admire, 'keep thinking good thoughts" until there is news once again from Wandaland where the cows are always hungry and never gets milked. That's all. kp

Teaching an Old Dog New Tricks

You have news from Wandaland where the cows are always hungry and not milked;

Who ever it was which said "you can't teach an old dog new tricks" probably didn't keep at it (trying) long enough. I would have to say "this person" may have let their mouth overload their as, uh "behind." (Like to have forgotten, Donna that I had promised to keep it clean) Anyway I have learned after a number of years of being exposed to loading a dishwasher, I've been sort of doing it wrong. Also there is always room for one more plate and cup.

Nay, the electric griddle you gave us a couple years ago sure is coming in handy. I can make pancakes the size of a plate or as small as "four bits" on it. You can sort of play around with pouring out the batter on the griddle, making breakfast a bit of fun too. If you pour the batter all in one place the pancake will be round, and 'bout as big as the plate when you keep pouring. You can pour out the batter such as to have a pancake which has a hand with fingers. Bet y'all didn't know all that. It doesn't take a whole lot of practice, but you probably shouldn't allow anyone to watch the first time because you might want to maintain you planned to have "scrambled pancakes."

Wanda has "ump-teen" number of sick day "on the books" but she went back to work Monday only after three days of convalescing at home. I drive her to work and back and sometimes it's like driving "Driving Miss Daisy and other times like driving Ms Bucket." It hasn't been much interesting hanging out at her office during the day as there is not much I can help with. Not a lot of magazines to look through and most have any pictures. She will not let me doing any of the bossing stuff there as she says it's her turf. I think that is her way of getting even with me. She hasn't threatened to fire me yet, but I'm not so sure you can free help.

A few days ago when I finished with all the "have to do" inside domestic chores I cared to doing at home, I went outside and just sit and did some thinking on a lot of stuff. Some folks claim they do their best thinking while sitting on "the throne", and others while lying back on a creek bank with an ole cane fishing pole watching the floater bob up and down in the water. The truth is I had been cooped up all morning in the house and could feel the cabin fever setting in. It was unusually warm that afternoon and it just so come to pass the side of the house which blocked the breeze was the "sunny side." I learned a long time ago when "the fever" commences to cause "everything to go wrong", its best to start taking the cure. Besides that, this kind of medicine is not so hard to get down.

I sat down in the one ornamental iron chair we have outside, and noticed immediately Ziggy the cat had found a warm spot there next to the house to sleep. Occasional she would sort of stretch and purr as if though dreaming of catching a fat mouse to eat.

Teaching an Old Dog New Tricks

Course Patches, the dog had to follow me around the house. It wasn't long before I was watching him creep along with his nose to the ground sniffing-out an earth worm or something to aggravate.

Dogs are a bit like people. Some are friendly and pretty while others are ugly and act as if thought they had a handful of "bitter pill" for breakfast or something.

What is it that causes us to wonder about stuff we wonder about? Could it be too much success, though little it may be, causes the real person inside to escape back to the simpler side of life?

I don't know a lot, actually nothing, about this kind of stuff. Someone has said "success brings out the real person", and when you think about it, it's probably right. And sometimes we don't "think much" of that real person either! So what is really success and the real person we wonder . . . Probably a good many people never get to be in life what they consider successful. Some rationalize the "why not" away, and others probably don't even like to think about such.

I got to wondering also if dads these days sometime carry their young sons down to the fire station, where some big tall fireman takes them by the hand and helps them in the driver's seat of a shinny red fire truck and even lets them wear a hat. Do little girl with pig tails think about kissing a frog and having it to turn into their handsome prince? There are still places up in the Midwest country where a boy wants "a girl just like the girl that married dear ole dad." I wondered if young girls still have a "hope chest" where they store treasures collected over the years just waiting for the time when there will be a cottage with a white picket fence.

Maybe it was the warm sun and last bit of coffee brought out in my "one of a kind cup" which cause me thinking on some of the good people that has been in my life. One such person was the high school principal who drove a bus, and also was the math teacher. He didn't believe so much in giving a lot of tests. He liked to send students to the black board and have them solve (work out) problems. Sometime he watched you every step of the way. He always gave me a C-plus no matter if I did all my homework and made an "A" on the short ten minute six-week test or solved problems on the black board.

It was after I had been in the navy when I managed the courage to ask him "why"! He gave me several reason "why" but the one I like the best was "you were always just a little better than that, but it kept you trying to do better." I'm thinking school is about trying harder on "how to be all that a person can be." School was a bit different back in the 30's and 40's. It was in high school math classes where we stood before other students and recited things as "Psalms 23, the Lord's Prayer, and The Ten Commandments." It was after being discharged from the navy that I learned my high school math teacher was also a Sunday school teacher, and I think a deacon in a church of his community. I "cringe" just thinking about how life might have been for me had it not been for people like him and my daddy.

I remembered quitting my work and coming home to spend a few day before leaving for the navy. As I was leaving that day Daddy called me aside and said "son don't forget what you have been taught at home." Well I am ashamed to say there were times of "forgetting!"

There is a Proverb in the Bible, in the Book of Proverbs, which states" train up a child in the way he should go and when he get old he want depart from it," or something having the same meaning. We may think since that is in the Bible, it has to be true, that is it has to happen. Well it is true alright, but we may observe it doesn't always happen. So what is going on here with Proverbs? I read some place where Biblical proverbs are words of wisdom from a wise person on how "things" normally are. The "outcome" of a proverb will usually be as given, but not necessarily always that way.

I thought about it having to be more than just pure luck why I am living today, and what has allowed me to "celebrate" a four score and ten, and a few more. Yes, it all has to do with a Proverb, with people who cared about other people. I wondered if I have cared as much as I should have. A wise older woman told me many years ago, when I became a proud member of the parenting society, that parents never become qualified until it is too late. I know this is true to some extent. A few years back I was talking to "my oldest" about "something", and was about "half-way" apologizing to her about some of my lack of parenting skills when she said "dad that's alright", that was because of "where you were at, at the time."

This is the stuff that's been bugging my mind the last few days here at Wandaland where he cows are always hungry and gives no milk. I'm riding on out of here. kp

ON RELATIONSHIPS

On two successive days I heard geese honking as they were passing overhead this past week. Each time I was sitting in a chair outside under a tree and could not see them. No way to know if they were flying north or south, east or west or if they were in a "V" formation or not. My farmers' almanac doesn't have anything to say about geese flying in January, so I suppose we will have to wait and see what Ole Phil, the groundhog has to say about winter coming on. I hear tell thousands of people make the pilgrimage each year in February to Pennsylvania to see the "little furry rascal." I wonder if candled are given to the people now days, probably not.

News from Wandaland where the cows are always hungry and never needs milking is a bit personal. Wanda's shoulder is giving her a lot of deep down despair, agony, grief and misery just about every few day now, and it appears she will have an operation on it soon. Just hope and pray it "turns out" better than my back operation. It was Ralph Marston who said "Each time you encounter a difficult situation, you have two basic choices, you can choose to deal with it or you can choose to let it deal with you." Or, was it Flip Wilson who said that? She has put off dealing with her misery and has decided "enough is enough", it's time to take control. Ignoring it hasn't made it go away but just worse so it seems.

Well our shed to park the golf cart in is coming along pretty good. That is, getting installed or constructed. I'm not too fast now days, and like to rest a lot I suppose. It sort of hurts when you miss a nail with the hammer and it lands without warning on a finger. Maybe, between finger smashes, it will be finished before too many more weeks go by, and without a lot more smashed figures, ha. No, I don't do golfing; we got the cart to ride around in here on the place. It is good to ride the fence lines with to see where they need mending. We have one darn ole big red heifer who likes to stay in practice pushing through fences. Much more of it and she could wind-up as hamburger on someone's plate! At the moment I can't carry a lot with me on the "Flint Stone Car" but I am going to enlarge the "carrying deck" in the back to hold more things, like maybe a snack and some cold drinks. It is handy to go to the mail box, which it is a good one half mile up on the main road where the mail rider drops off our mail.

The Flint Stone Car has a lot of batteries under the seat which powers the engine. We are glad it is not gasoline driven due to the possibility of somehow setting the grass on fire.

A cyber-pal has sent me a lot or interesting reading by Ralph Marston. As many of you probably know his writing are in the "Daily Motivator", which some of you have probably subscribed to at one time or another. His is "good stuff" and if you have a few minutes to feed your mind with inspiring thoughts, there is only one other better source, that being the Holy Bible. I suppose that most people who get the News from Wandaland like to think they are "religious", and that a number probably have their "quite time" for devotional reading. As to me, I am "off and on" about reading the Bible and not so much proud about being off so much either.

I suppose what I had wanted or started to say about Ralph Marston's literature is that it contains a lot of practical applications of Biblical teachings. Here is some of it, so see what it reminds you of. "Your priorities are determined not by what you say they are but by what you are willing to pay for them." "It's easy to say you have certain dreams, goals and ambitions. It takes more than just claiming to have a dream if that dream is to be realized." Darn good physiology for the secular mind or spiritual wisdom for the religious minded, don't you think?

Did a real stupid thing a day or two ago by turning on the T.V. to hear news that I did not want to hear in the first place. I wonder why I was tempted to do that, and just why I allowed myself to be overcome by such temptations. Where a needle would be stuck if it were possible to give the world a "shot" to cure all the wrong "doings" going on? What have we humans gravitated to when we use disasters and other peoples misfortunes for our own personal gain and profit? Billions have been paid for false claims of Katrina damages, to people who never suffered any damage what so ever, according to reports. I suppose that people are tempted to the good things as well as to the bad things, and hopefully it is more to the good things, but not a lot of that ever "makes" the news.

A few nights ago I went down to the Stump water grocery store in Prairieville to where there was to be a neighborhood meeting. I wanted to hear the people that came engage in their rhetoric of various varieties. They did, and a few shifted into overdrive once in a while. One ole gal could crank it up to 40 words a second and possible gust up to 60. She could raise the decibel level in the room to a thundering roar. As you might expect mostly those who were there were older people like me who probably had nothing better to do than go and contribute their "two cents worth" of useless conversation. The county commissioner for the precinct, who is up for reelection, was there and told the people all the good stuff he had been doing for them. There were two or three persons who thought it a good idea to incorporate into a small town. The guy who made the suggestion probably wanted to be mayor, ha. I guess the most significant thing said was by a man letting it be known his Coon Dog had died. I think these meeting takes place once a month, so if they have not "petered out" I might find myself there again in six month or so to catch-up on what has been happening in the neighborhood.

I picked up a rather old copy of the "God Old Days" magazine which had been "kicking around" the room for some time. In fact it come out in October of 2002. I glanced through several of the short stories wanting to see why it was that I had been keeping it around for so long. It might have been that I was saving it because of an intriguing story "My Angel" by Lilah Archambeault Eick. It was about a time when she was nine years old and decided to run away from home because her mother had scolded her for not changing school clothes and doing her chores. I recon that most kids have "been there and done that" at one time in their life.

When I was about nine and probably in about the second grade (as old lady Johnson had failed me in first grade) I only had two pairs of overalls to were to school. It was "a given" to change into patched work overalls the first thing after getting off the bus.

Next was to look for a snack which was usually cold biscuits and sorghum syrup left over from breakfast. We always had chores! Daddy and Mama apparently believe strongly "an idle mind is the devil's work place." There was a lot of "busy work" in those days as well as some meaningful kind. I just never "saw" any good reason to be pulling up bitter weeds, or cutting down persimmon sprouts. I remember once when I decided to run away from home too. It was kind of early in the dark part of the night. I got a little way from the house and got afraid and came back.

Running away from home as a kid seems like "such a childish thing" to do. Yet, this is something teenagers do and even grown married people as well as little kids. When we think about it, people be they little boys and girls or older people, don't run away from food and a warm place to sleep; we run away from relationships. A relationship usually happens between people who "rub elbows" and the good ones don't usually happen. Good relationships have to be cultivated, watered and fertilized if they are to grow and be meaningful. I guess that moms and dads who are busy raising a family don't feel like they have time to "slowing down" a lot and just be a good friend. This is the kind of stuff that doesn't ever wear out, and is free, but costly designer "britches" lasts only a season. So until next time, that's all the news from Wandaland, where the cows are always hungry, never needs milking, where Patches the dog is always competing for attention. kp

Keeping Up Appearances

Hello everybody, you have e-mail news from Wandaland where the cows are always hungry, never needs milking and where Ole Patches guard the place out by the road. "They" tell me Mother Nature came visiting in these parts a few days ago officially opening spring. It was the day we got a "frog-strangling" down pour which filled up all the cracks in the ground and a few of the stock ponds in these parts. Then a day or so afterwards the mercury dropped making it at least a "two-dog" night. Well, anyway it is the start of the season where you go to the local nursery walk through the place looking at all the pretty flowers and sort of plan in your mind where you could put them in the yard. As you load up the cart it suddenly "hits you", these "beauties" have to be put in the ground with you supplying the muscle, so about half of them go back on the rack. You come home with only one flat more than there are places to set them out. But what about the fertilizers? Ah yes, spring time when mamas everywhere lets their kids kick off their shoes and play out in the yard bare foot, running and carrying on like wild Indians.

It will not be long now until Easter will be upon us. It is the most important religious holiday of Western Christianity (and others perhaps). It celebrates the resurrection of Jesus Christ without which life would be meaningless. The Easter season for some believers (or churches) is fifty days of fasting whereby it ends on Pentecost. I believe some churches refer to this fifty day of fasting as Lent. I suppose that most everyone is familiar with "Palm Sunday", "Ash Wednesday", "Good Friday" as well as "Easter Morning." Here in America (and other countries as well) Easter has been secularized to a large degree with things as colored eggs supposedly hidden about by a Bunny. It is a time for ladies to have a new "spring outfit", little girls new bonnets and slippers. It is a special time everyone looks forward to immensely, no matter the reason.

Most of you know I have a daughter and son-in-law who live in Tulsa, well occasionally. Since before Christmas last year we have been trying to get away to go see them, and we finally "got it together!" (That is when they would be home and no loose ends here at Wandaland to attend to.) Better yet Wanda "rode shotgun" all the way there and back and never once, mind you, started to act like Ms Bucket on "Keeping Up Appearances." I think the kids have done took leave of their senses! They are drinking bottled water which comes from Fiji Island. I couldn't resist taking a swig, so I did and it taste the same as the water Wal Mart sells which is bottled in Fort Worth, Texas. I can say this , it comes in a prettier decorated square bottle.

The trip to Renee's was kind of a short one, and maybe that is the best kind. However we did get in a little playing Mexican Trash Train and go to P.F. Chaing for some Orange Peel Shrimp and Lettuce wrap. Renee is in the "mist" of doing a receipt book of some of her gourmet cooking. We had some pecan pie which she made and I wouldn't be surprised if it shows up in the book as it was some good! I am talking having a second helping of it. They are also leaving in a few days for Cook Islands. It's to be a vacation as well as looking into building or buying a resort there.

T. J. was to leave early Monday morning, like 4:30 A.M. to carry one of the cats for some treatment at a hospital over in Kansas. Another thing (which I don't quite grasp) is they are planning on selling their house in Tulsa and moving back to the "Hill Country" of Texas very soon.

A couple years ago Renee installed a Web-site for the Parker-Pool families here each person could list the kind of gift they hoped to receive for Christmas. Well as our little toaster-oven was get a little sluggish about making the second round of toast and slow in cooking those can biscuits, I listed a toaster as something I wanted. Renee, Wanda and I thank you for getting it for us, and it works well. Had I known we were getting it I would have consented to it being sent at Christmas. It is one of those convection multi-racks baking, toasting, broiling and keeping warm ovens. There is even a place on the box it came in where you can push and the box will talk telling "stuff" about the darn thing. We could hardly wait to get back home and try it out. It was on page nine where you read about making toast. It may take a whole lot of reading and practice to "get used to it." I told Wanda as she was flipping though the pages hunting for how to make toast it appeared to be as difficult learning to operate as the VCR recording machine was. There is even a page or two of instructions on what to do in case of a "food flare-up." I was to learn that means if the food starts to burn with flames just unplug it, leave the door shut and do not squirt water on it. Like I told Wanda a few weeks ago, we need to get "out there" more and see all the gadgets the rest of the world has.

That's 'bout all the news from Wandaland where the cows are always hungry and never needs milking, where Patches greets all visitors with a friendly bark and a wagging tail. So until next time be as a good cyber-pal says "keep thinking those good thoughts." kp

Moving on up to the West Side

Come now and listen up you'll rowdy friends and relatives on account of this here are news from Wandaland where the cows are always hungry, never get milking, and Ziggy the mealy-mount, no account, good for nothing cat no longer wants an improved relationship with her benefactor, namely me. She is one darn moody cat! That old liver-lipped cat has taken to walking around and looking at me like just who in nail do you think you are, anyhow. "One of these days, Ziggy!" Well at least the weather aint halfway bad but the cooler weather seems to have caused them cows to graze on the hay a lot more. That too is Okay as hay was plentiful and at a good price this year.

Now it done appears if I have got moved into the 21st century even with me screaming and kicking my feet on account of not wanting to be saddled with all those gadgets what turns on the folks who come from the loins of those who are known as the "baby boomer." As George, as in Mr. Jefferson would said, I've moved on up. I done had me one of those cell phone. Since it was a present from "you know who", and it came with getting learning up on it from you know who also. I had to Oooh and Ah over it some. Now it seems this gadget does a lot more that sends my talking and listens to y'll talk. Man I can take pictures, get my email on it, get music, get every kind of conversion known under the sun. To boot it has big push buttons numbers that you don't have to have tooth picks to punch up the numbers. Then those great big numbers appear on the screen too and ye don't even have to have a spy glass to see em. Now aint all that something Vern?

Now if that don't get your goat or shorts in a tight wad giving you wedges, then this will. I got laid on me one of them there GPS thing what done told me where I am at and how to get to where I don't know to git thr. It is like the phone by having a lot of other useless stuff to get your mind all befuddled and stuff. I am talking gadgets so complicated that it will take a 5 year old to master them, well maybe they would have a good shot at it.

Now I can pack the darn phone around, hanging on my suspenders, so as to let the world know "I have arrived." I can even go in my favorite restaurant and commence to annoy others by calling all y'all and running my mouth to you about my pending hemorrhoid procedure. That aught to raise an eye brow or two. There are a few other choice things I am giving thought to as to sharing with y'all about.

Just as soon as I can find out what my number is I will let y'all know so that y'all who done got them "called I.d." can reject my calls.

Well as y'all can tell, Tim, I done made out like I don't know how. Recon I'll be learning up on that and warming up to all the credit card bills when they get here in a month or two.

There is one other piece of good news, for me that is, but probably too good no for some of you. I got me one of those battery powered chair so that I can run around in places like Disney World and Moody Gardens. I had to trade in the Cadillac for a van so as to haul it places. Also got a crane installed in the back which will lift it up and suck it on inside for hauling around. Now what are "they" going to think of next? I am starting to believe that people really did go to the moon. Now folks that is how it has been around here at Wandaland where the cows are always hungry and never get milk, for milk, uh what else could it be? kp

Hiring A Head Coach

Hello folks, it is time to sit a spell. Go get yourself a dipper of cool water from the well as you catch up on the latest from Wandaland where the cows are always hungry and never get milked.

All coins have two sides, and usually they are different except for those used to snicker someone in a coin toss. Often times the different sides are referred to as "heads and tails." In as much legitimate coins have differences on opposite side we sometime speak of an issue having a different and opposite point of view than what may have been expressed.

Not so long ago there was "talk" about the name "French Fries" here in the United States became known as "Home Fries." My take on the matter was some people felt we should not as much acknowledge France because of none support of what our government was engaged in. Just where would we be had it not been for the French lending a hand when the colonies was unable to gain independence without their help? It was the French who made the gift to this young nation of the "Statue of Liberty" which is a monument of what this nation is all about.

Now on to other concerns! It appears to me written on those thin pages of a book named Revelation of my King James authorized Bible there is a lot of "fast forwarding" taking place to where it is written at the end "Come, Lord Jesus." Calamities and disastrous events are happening all over the world at a rate they overlap. No sooner does a pot hole gets patched another one appears where the foundation of democracy commences to erode.

There is a lot of "Monday Morning Quarterbacking" taking place after the fact. We wonder why the coach and coaching staff could not look ahead and see the consequences of "plays" ran. Perhaps the same can be said of country's coach, the staff, and the supreme referees in those "yester years."

It is believed this nation was founded on religious principals. It has been, and perhaps still is a nation of great wealth. All them books in the front of the Bible seem to teach wealth is to be shared with less fortunate. The other side of that coin is seen by many that our nation has engaged in buying so called friendship. It is believed by many people the United States has lost its world influence. Yes, we are in a sore lagging economy, a time of depression for the general population.

In my life time there has been erosion which brought about three recessions where there was a demand by the population there be a change in the "coach and staff." Not a lot was said in the way of the supreme referees, or the attitude and actions of the people attending the game.

Onward to the "nitty-gritty" before you locate the off switch. It is not very long now until our nation will be electing a "head coach." What will be the criteria for hiring? Will it be an embellished resume? Will it be someone who has the better ability to read speeches wrote for them from a "teleprompter?" Will it be because many people feel it is time that race and sex matter? Will it be someone whom public opinion has determined has the proven qualifications in all areas of the "big game" to be won; someone who knows a lasting "win win" results from the "old fashion way" of statesmanship, instead of pleasing words?

There is probably much truth in "be careful what you truly go after" on account it just might come to pass. Another providential statement is "it is not a good idea to catch a tiger by its tail." Are there members of an organized society who will cast their vote for someone who is a convicted embezzler to be their treasure? Do people in a happy neighborhood allow child molesters to live among them? No accusation is being made or intended. Ambitions and goals are often the "corner stone" of a foundation built on rock as well as those built on sand . . .

That is how I see it here at Wandaland where the cows are always hungry, don't ever get milked, and I am hopeful our little patch of real estate will continue to have good grazing. So until next time y'all keep a smile on your faces and a melody in your hearts. kp

Hindrance to Life

Hello everyone, it is a mighty fine day here at Wandaland where the cows are always hungry, never get milked and where Ole Patch the "the Blue Tick Hound" done went on a strike of wagging his tail.

It makes no "never mind" what sod you travel as there are things "out there" we humans tend to recognize as annoyances and some as destructive to our lives. I guess we shouldn't be thinking like that about creatures God has put here on this planet. Back in "olden days" (Nay & Tim) when I was supposed to be a field engineer working out on Yuma desert of Arizona we had to watch-out for Sidewinder Snakes. They don't crawl like other snakes but have a side crawl for better locomotion I suppose. I just know you do not step out of a car at night without first shining a light about.

Down in Bayou country of Louisiana there are/were Nutrias running around all over the swamps and roads, which are fury little rascals that looks like a super sized rat. I am told they have teets on their backs. I have never heard of one figuring us humans to be their enemy and wanting to leave battle marks about our ankles. Then in Texas there is the Armadillo but you don't see a lot of them anymore. It seems like the Skunks have taken over. There once was a joke about Armadillos where it was said the reason why a chicken crossed the road was to show the Armadillo it could be done without getting ran over. There is a stretch of road between Baton Rouge and New Orleans which would become slick during crawfish migration with dead crawfish. People who live in California get concerned at times about their state falling off in the ocean. Then along the gulf coast from Brownsville to the tip of Florida people board up and leave for hurricanes, and here in Texas we run and get in the storm cellars when the clouds looks like a tornado is forming.

Well, I do not take a liking to piss ants, red bugs, ticks and other kinds of creepy-crawlers bugs in the little world. Bees, hornets and wasp are high on my don't fool with list too. However, pretty girls are still at the top of my like list. Recon it is time to be closing the barn door here at Wandaland where the cows are always hungry and never gives up their milk. kp

Inventions

Some of you may recall the time when you made a purchase in a store and the sales person wrote it up, sent it with you money or check in a vacuum tube upstairs. In a short while your receipt and change as appropriate returned in the tube. There were actually "floor walkers" who assisted you to departments and kept "an eye" on customers. Five and Ten Cents stores sold many five and ten cent items, and sometime these stores might be referred to as "racket stores", I suppose because of the noise of the customers. It was a time when there were very few to non manikins to model men and women's underwear. There were "certain other things" kept under the counter, usually at "drug stores", as they were called more so than pharmacies, and had to be asked for.

Hello Folks, this is Wandaland from over here where the cows are always hungry and never gets milking; where Patches the dog thinks his reason to be here is to guard the house and Ziggy, the cat allows mice to molest her as she likes to sleep all day.

Well, I remember many years ago when computers mostly used "CPM" and only a few used the Micro Soft DOS. If you wanted a Modem, it had to be purchase separately. Web sites to visit were scares as hen's teeth. Then one day there was a standardizing of DOS and it made lots of computer obsolete. Then they come for "build in" modems, and operating system such as "Windows." We no longer had to remember all of those DOS commands. I suppose this was to computers as automatic transmissions were to vehicles.

The automobiles stick shift protruded from the floor was a long shaft with a knob and there were foot operated starters, and light dimmers on the floor board as well. The freight train which came through Cushing once a day was a coal burning steam engine pulling a few cars. The freight was mostly pulp wood, or perhaps tomatoes or bales of cotton when in season. It is hard to imagine there is a group of young growing up who can not "fathom" a time when there was not instant communications to any place in the world. There is instant access to just about any information one would like to know about. Telephone companies in days gone by were mostly small locally owned. At first there were no numbers to dial. To use the phone you turned a crank to ring the operator and got connected to your party. Many people had "party lines", even in large towns. I remember listening to people carrying on a conversation on the party line. I also recall being told "get off the line" numerous times as well.

There has been many, and I am "talking many" wonderful inventions made quite available which has become just part of an accepted way of life. Not only is there cells phone, there are things such as washing machine, driers, microwaves, color television, riding mowers, weed eaters, sprinklers, home security systems, and on we can go. Did I mention home computers which can operate very quickly while holding literally thousands of files? Once the old tail dragging DC3 two engine prop airplane was the best there was. As the Pilgrim would say "its mind boggling."

It is frequently said no one like to make a mistake, and that is generally true I suppose. It is also believed that many people will not admit their mistakes and, that too is most likely correct. I suppose that normal human beings will not admit to subconscious thoughts of being correct in most all things they engage in. Making mistakes is just as much a part of living as attempting to "batting a hundred" when up to bat. Some people will say "life is a gamble" possibly meaning there are chances to take in life if one will ever attain. Perhaps the biggest mistake of all a person can make is to do nothing for fear of doing something wrong. There is another familiar old saying which says something like "it is better to have loved and lost, and to not have loved at all." I just happen to have acquaintances who have lost in loving and vow they will never "fall in love again."

Wandaland's Horse Fancy

You know, when a cowboy gets his seat vacated by a horse, he may think twice before crawling back on but, get back on he will do, though with much caution of being "throw off" once again. Just how often and why will a person "throw in the towel" in the ring of life and not come out swinging before the whistle is blown for ending the last round?

It has been said people should plan to make a mistake or two in various aspects of life, so when it happen it becomes the "spoon full of sugar which makes the medicine go down in a more delightful way." Perhaps so, and then again not is my thought on the matter. We should always be ready to recognize our mistakes and not allow our springs to get wound up so tight there is an explosion over them." I guess that is pretty hard to do some times and, it may take a long time to get unwound over some things. I remember once, a long time ago, deciding to take a train ride to New Orleans. As it turned out it was a terrible mistake for a number of reason. I must have told my self a thousand times during the trip and for a while afterwards "I can't believe I have done this." Needless to say, I couldn't "let go" of it because of thinking I could have never been as foolish as that! Not letting go is sinful vanity and when one can not believe they are capable of doing regrettable things, they are self deceived. Well, vanity and self deception are oftentimes results of not "letting go" of mistakes made.

Let me ask you, when you do something "real stupid" such as pouring salt in a glass of iced tea instead of sugar" do you lecture yourself, or do you laugh at yourself? I think so many time we fail to put "thing" in their proper perspective. Taking the train to New Orleans only "warped my personality" for the moment. It had nothing to do with shaping "world history", or "stunting the growth" of my young son. Perhaps you may be a person who enjoys reading the book of Proverbs in the Christian Bible. If so, you have probable read where we are to learn from our own mistakes, also to observe the mistakes of others and profit from them.

Probably most people have a concept and know the meaning of the word "mistake." Like so many other words its exact meaning is more or less determined in what context it is used in. However, the one word which seems to define it is simply "wrong." When we give thought to "mistakes" I think it could be said that mistakes, in general, are made as a result of a wrongful decision, judgment, assumption, or some other wrongful or imperfect thought.

I suppose where "the rubber hits the road" so to speak, mistake is a relative to an absolute. Now if that is the case, and it probably is, then a mistake may not always be a mistake, if that makes any sense to you. Mistakes have to be judged against some intended outcome. Often times we may examine a particular action, or course taken, not having any expectation of the outcome. In other words we do things not considering the outcome of our actions. How about the last time you attempted to do something good for someone and it failed, was that a mistake? Now that is a "big can of worms" to open up!

Thoughts should lead us to asking ourselves if it is wrong to fail. Course that question has to be qualified. Most people would say it is wrong to fail (neglect) when there is opportunity and good reason to act otherwise. Let us never forget things which may constitute neglect for someone could very well be intentional with another person.

Needs which help constitute our physic, things we promote and allow to become important in life will often times determine behavior.

Life is good here at Wandaland where the cows are always hungry and never gives up their milk. Have stiff to do, will catch you later. kp

A SENTIMENTAL JOURNEY

You have "News from Wandaland" where the cows are always hungry and never milked, where the blue tick dog named Patches guards the place and "Mealy mouth cat named Ziggy" is always out in the field hunting for a mouse. A very special greeting to new friends in Australia, New Zealand, Nova Scotia, Snowbirds up north and east USA, Southerners in the US and those in the land of the mid-night sun

First perhaps I should say who is sending you this news. Kodell and Wanda Parker from Texas living on a 30 acre farm with a few cows, about 60 miles east of Dallas, Texas where it gets "powerfully" hot in summer time and often times gets a few degrees below freezing in the dead of winter.

Please know that I consider our trek to the "last frontier" and on in to the wilderness of the Yukon will be an experience which will live on in memory for Wanda and me. We sincerely believe it will be so for everyone. It was absolutely amazing that everyone was extremely friendly and thoughtful of each other. I have to conclude there were no Baptist people among us, ha.

Our House Wilderness St, Anch, Ak

Having lived in Alaska for several years and visited the Yukon occasionally I can say we were "smiled upon" with the weather, as the temperature didn't require layers, and there was hardly ever a cloud in the sky except sometime over some mountains. Was not our Tour Director Colleen great with looking after us, also her knowledge of pertinent things? She never lost a bag or anyone who belonged to them. Bill, the coach driver is deserving of some accolades as well. I have to admit the "farewell dinner" at the Alaska Princess Hotel was a bit moving as we hugged and said our "goodbyes" and best wishes as we had truly became community for a short time.

There is an "old saying" there is a mattress sale somewhere all the time and that traveling via air in the coach section there is always a crying baby due to their ears hurting. Folks the part about babies is only a proverb. We had not one going or returning. Actually I think it would have been great to hear a baby cry for me, but not the baby, which would have lessend the boring trips. All the flight was as smooth as a new baby's butt.

I have a few pictures when Alaska was not overrun with people and would be glad to share them with anyone who would like to have them. There are several pictures in the Yukon as well.

So for now I will say "happy trails" to everyone and really look forward to hearing from each one. It may be a while before getting back to you as I had about 200 new emails upon returning home.

Renee, Wanda and I appreciate the gifts you and T.J. presented to us for the trip and I can say it put the icing on the cake. The big box of things which came last evening was received with much surprise and awe. I am thinking we will be enjoying all the "goodies" with the relatives, and certainly do appreciate your thoughtfulness in the matter. I just have to say you "supersized" it more than just a little, and Wanda and I are truly grateful for all you kids have done.

Diane said on the trip that she had a gift for Jack, and I will send it with the bib for Jack. Y'all take care, and hope you get to feeling better. Love and best wishes from Wanda and me. As to the cows, they are out to pasture for nibbling. kp

A VISIT TO THE DOCTOR

You have news from Wandaland where we really do feed the cows, take no milk leaving it for their little ones.

It was yesterday when I sort of "took leave of myself" while waiting an hour or so in the doctor's examine room for those mortal words "your tests were all okay." I have faults, I really do! How I know is because my squeeze gives me that "evil look" now and again.

Yep, it was yesterday when I started to get irritated about having to sit there all alone when one of those pretty, wonderful, charming nurses could have kept me company and kept me from having a chip on the shoulder. Here it is I am having bad thought when I should have been counting my blessings. It is suggested by people we deserve better, but do we? I don't know, but probably not. I think we might deserve better than the wait which could possible be in store.

I tried to amuse myself by looking at all the inside body parts of the man on the wall. I am thinking a couple of reasons why doctors have to go to doctoring school so long is learn how to pronounce all those parts, and how to write their name such as baby scribbling. It didn't take more than a couple minutes to get bored with that. Then my thoughts turn to sort of rearranging all the stuff on the counter and some of the furniture. Something must have kicked in on account of I thought it best not to do that.

There were a few magazines and I was a bit reluctant to handle them as they could have germs on them and I didn't come there to get germs. I kind of look at them anyway but cease because there was none about "girls stuff."

Now I know to some of you this will come as a surprise; I have other defects than being irritable and impatient. I really do, I have one more for sure and that is not having what grandpa called "gumption" (that is a country folk talk for city talk "good sense.") I never had the gumption to save any of those "Little Lu Lu" comic books. Yeah, having a hip pocket full of them and Captains Marvel to trade was some of those good old days. Learning how to smoke corn silks out behind the barn and other "right of passage" help make for good old days.

Well, anyhow I finally sailed out of the waiting room to the nurse station and told her I am ready for the doc to see me. I was sort of hoping she would say will I do but she didn't. All she had to say was trot on back to the room like a good boy and behave. I still say some folks can't seem to take a joke. This was not my primary doctor. My primary doctor is a lady doctor and I like lady doctors because they will cut you some slack when men doctors won't. Actually my medicine woman that I had a crush on left me to go back to practice up north.

Well I need to go dust off a saddle blanket and rake out the barn some and some other piddling stuff, maybe like wonder off down to Wally World and race someone in a cart or have a hotdog with mustard at the deli or something another. Until the net bring news again from Wandaland where the cows are now fed all y'all keep on grunting. kp

JUST HANGING OUT

Life is like shore 'nough good here at Wandaland even if the cows are always hungry and don't give up their milk. I still have man's best friend to ride shotgun with me on the improved Flint-stone when a notion is taken to take it out and ride fences for a spell.

When mentioning life is good I am talking like goodlier even if the cows are on a strike like forever against management for more hay. Every day is like a holiday here among the overgrown bushes some people calls trees where rabbits don't worry about being chased. Icing on the cake is every day is like a holiday and the grub is fitting for a king. Loving my squeeze is a big kick like as if I was a Sooner.

Now the big reason why I am jawing to all y'all again on a quick turnaround is to declare my dragging on down to Wally World yesterday. Sometime I get a hankering to go there with no purchase in mind and so it happened.

Passing up getting sheared there at the place which has a Barbara pole that aint worked in a coon's age I put the peddle to the metal and cruised on to the place where there is good trolling. After circling the lot a time or two looking for a good place to land I finally tie up about a rock's throw from the automatic gate.

I didn't foot it with the few stragglers and strays taking stuff back on account it didn't fancy them, just strolled on without becoming community where I had to restrain myself from. Anyhow, I made it to the front there were people sit on a bench sometimes for various and sundress reason. I notice this female, oh I guess she was much younger than she looked. It was that kind of look when a horse is road hard over rugged terrain and not cooled down properly.

It appeared that she threw me a smile like an invite to sit a spell so I don't do no culling, just take what is offered. I don't know, she, it or whatever, may have just been "panhandling" or smooching for change to buy some Ripple.

Well I sat down but not so close to have little creep crawler things exit her and find better grazing. Now I don't mean to be "high hating" or anything like that. I have been there a time or two myself.

I was lucky though on account a big wig from one of those terrible oil company who is responsible for all the holes in the ozone done came along while I was once sitting on a bench looking like that. There I was, sitting down to keep from falling down and had my hat off when a few people came by and dropped a few coins in it.

What I started to jaw about was this big wig came along, stopped and said "fellow you look like to me you would make a cost planner for our company, wouldn't happen to be down on your luck would you? Actually this is a story for another time, but I just wanted to say I don't go around high-hating nobody. That was a long time ago when work came to you and a different administration was in control.

I looked at this "what ever" who had a couple of little boulders in a holder and smiled back and introduced myself as Mr. Wonderful from, well you guessed it. It wasn't like I had cheating on my squeeze or stuff like that on my mind, I just want to let her (her as I finally concluded) she could still have faith in humanity. Besides, if anyone should know that I am old and harmless well it is, you guess again. It is hard sometime to tell if someone is a female or a male with so many hippies, or yuppies or whatever with long hair and girl people that don't have much of a milk factory.

I am not the greatest person in the world to strike up jawing with folks I don't know, and was at loss how to wade in. I said looks like you are taking it easy. Her reply sort of put me at ease on account of she said "honey that is the only way I can take it any more." Recon that was just her way of saying she had a million mile of ruff road on her.

It could have been because I looked pretty shabby myself that she smiled and she hair looked like one of those person they show on channel four in the morning, like a whirlwind buzzed over for a while.

I could not but help noticing that a few of her teeth was missing and one or two looked like they were about decayed as much as possible and still hang in there. Not wanting her to feel bad or telling me to "buzz off" I said you must have been a very busy lady (I didn't say at what) to not have time to see "Painless Parker." All of the dam Yankee donkey and elephants know who that is, and when she said "I recon so" that was a clue.

She said I see you had lot of time to cohort with dentist as you don't have any choppers at all. I said yeah I see you have started to take notice of me about what I aint got no more. I told her that me and my squeeze are into gumming it now day. She said y'all do have no falsies? I told her yeah we do, but today is an even day and my squeeze has them on even days and me on odd days. I don't think I was very convincing about that because she just sort of frowned and then sort of smiled saying "now are you the luck one."

Well it finally happened; I got hit-up for a hamburger. I asked her if that was all that she was hungry for and she said for the moment. I had no idea what level this woman wanted to carry the jawing to and neither did I, so it was time to comment a little about the weather. I was asked if we always had weather like this which was another clue. This woman was starting to be seen as a lady who once had a lot of class as well as humor.

We went on in and to the back of Wally Word where there is one of those places you can get a veggie sandwich on Rye. We stopped a couple times going on back to look at stuff acting as if we had known each other for ever.

We got one of those foot long things and shared it at a table. I asked her if I could buy her a drink and she said that would be delightful. I asked what kind did she prefer and I was told a Margarita but it doesn't appear they might have it. I told her yep, that is right, today is Wednesday and they are not into that on Wednesday. I also said if you are serious about that maybe I can leave the cows and get back down here tomorrow and get you one. Her reply was she would have to wait and see what was penciled on her calendar for tomorrow.

She had earlier said her name was Marline or was it Marylyn. Anyway she went to the ladies power room back in the rear of the store and was there for a while. I did not recognize her when she came out. All the pancake stuff was off, hair back in place and didn't have the shuttled look. I said what in the world is going on here to which she replied, don't you know?" Nope I said. Well I am an under cover agent looking for someone that you resemble, but you are not that person. We left the store and I complimented her by stating she had undoubtedly been taken by some city slicker and she replied no not yet.

I had picked up a bouquet of flowers for my squeeze and when I got home she wanted to know what I had been up today. I told her nothing much; I know I could not say that I had not been gone for a long time because the car hood was warm and that is a dead give away.

Lets see, seem like I may have got into a corner with no way out unless I say Patches, the ole blue tick hound barked and shocked me away from daydreaming. Life is good here at Wandaland where the cows are always hungry and plum stingy about giving out their milk. kp.

Stop the World and Let Me Off

Many people seemingly feel as if there is no immediate hope for "having a good day" as they are struggling just to have a day! Good day folks, better yet have yourselves a wonderful day. You are now in the paddock of Wandaland where the cows are always hungry, and where I am wondering what it would be like if the late Edward "Eddy" Arnold had got someone to stop the world and had I got off.

The American Dream has perhaps for its foundation free enterprise with supply and demand being regulating factors in decades of the past. An honest day's pay for and honest day of work seems to be "out the window" having multi-supporting causes. There are those who's "American Dream" have circumvented natural and man made laws allows the wealthy to become wealthier, and the poor to live in a state of poverty. Success, with respect to earthly life is to gain more, and more and more. The American Way for many people, in all kinds of things, is to find ways to beat "the system", to find and take advantage of "loop holes" in well intended laws.

With all the many devastating things happening of late, a few things become "old hat" and forgotten. It seems like "light years" ago when the Mayor of New York City said pot holes in their streets were as much their way of life as other things. Certainly 9-11, and other cataclysmic events have brought about much change in the lives of people in the United States of America. Younger people are wondering perhaps "what is down the road" with respect to the "American Way?"

What will pay for a checked bag on an airline, or buying a ticket according to one's weight open the door for, if anything"? The principal is perhaps you pay for what you use and not that of someone else use. Some states prefer a sales tax over an income tax to help support their state government as this is seen as a fair way. A person who is insured in a group insurance does not pay according to respective use but that of the average. Old g-grandparents who haven't had a child in school in decades pay school taxes simply because they were enterprising enough to have real property. Of course all people benefits from schools, churches etc., but who benefits the most? I came from a large family of school children and our neighbor had only one child in school.

School tax evaluation was biased on property owned. Our neighbor was a "share cropper." My dear wife and I eat at a buffet frequently and times were I did my best to "get my money's worth." I no longer "pig out" on account I need to loose weigh as I plan to fly next year. Noticed one airline stopped handing out pretzels.

In time there may be "pay toilets" on airplanes and butt wipes (toilet paper) cost according to use as a way for airlines to recover individual use cost. Course they could also install condom vending machines in the toilet as well.

We wonder what effects if anything population growth and extended life age will have on future generations. Will Government Social Security be gradually "phased out?" The "American Way" seemingly is to grumble and tolerate small changes, even to basic freedoms. How much longer will it be before a small minority of employed people will be supporting the large majority of retired people? Certainly current laws prevent a hindrance to population growth such as China has. Are "stimulus checks" biased on income tax paid the fair way to help poverty level people? Lots of complex issues to the life for future generations to be sorted, much of which it is said is being passed on. Who is he or she who desires to be President and for what motivating purpose? My guess is President Bush has a secrete wish someone else had won the last term of the Presidency.

Out of the mouth of babes (young children) oftentimes comes wisdom. Many things in life we enjoy have reasons to no longer be enjoyed. I was reminded, "Don't be sad it ended, but be glad it all took place." Thank God for children's faith and optimism.

Various harmful drugs which could once be obtained by mail order was attempted to be regulated by taxation. The same kind of regulation was attempted in the use of whiskey. Current laws apparently prohibit "outlawing" the use of tobacco products. Tobacco is being attempted controlled by methods which have not worked in the past. Taxes have become an inexhaustible source of revenue so it seems to fix broken things. A hard lesson to learn is a country or person can not spend their way out of debt, and borrowing from "Peter to pay Paul" doesn't fix a root cause.

One last thought before throwing the switch, "will there soon come a time when "bottled water" will be more expensive than a Wine Cooler? Water we **need** an abundant supply; gasoline not so much of, so says Wandaland where the cows are always hungry and never get milked. I'm out of here kp

Spreading the Wealth

Hello friends and kin all over, you have news from Wandaland where the cows are always hungry and they are never milked.

London Leaves are still falling and the Lineman for the county has climbed a few more poles, but there is a whiff of odorous in the air. Yesterday's new was all about preparing to spread the wealth around. We had a missionary from South Africa to visit our church Sunday and his message was on national repentance. According to his schedule he has and will be speaking in several large churches across the nation before returning back to Cape Town. As Earnest would say Vern aint that something? Times were when this country sent missionaries to reform Africa. Well as I understand this part of Africa was under British rule for years.

Oh it was also mentioned in the news that the rich people are still at "bailing out" the rich. Several more billion was given to the American Investment Group (AIG) to prop up foreign countries who had invested here in buying up the country. I received an email a day or so ago where congress is "exploring" taxing (again) IRA's , 401K's, CD's and others saving of working people. A friend of ours who retired a year or so ago from an electric company had his retirement invested and lost it in the big swindle and he has had to find work again. I suppose he is one of the lucky ones as he was able to find employment to make "ends meet".

There is some good news here at Wandaland where the cows are always hungry and never gets milked. It has rained and rained, and more rain just about all night. Looking out the window to the pasture (paddock) it looks a bit like we might be Noah's Ark in the mist of a world wide flood. The good things are, we needed the rain a lot as stock tanks are low and we got a lot of winter hay staged before the staging area became to wet to go there.

Wanda kept making Z's this morning while the earth was being dumped on. I had breakfast of Jimmy Dean sausage and Ms "B" biscuits piping hot when she finally got her working parts to working and got up on "the right side" of the bed. Had some eggs out ready to crack and build them over easy on account she likes them that way, but no eggs this morning. We had sausage biscuits accented with fig preserves one of my sisters gave me for such an occasion.

MSN stuck it to me again. This time they wiped out some of my stuff, and when they put it back, I had wished they had not. I had up close to 10, 000 emails in my sent folder and about the same in my inbox. Man, I am telling you that a number of them went back a lot of coon ages. Some of the stuff looked a bit interesting as I had forgotten them, so I just added a bunch of folders and put them in to look at later, well perhaps. Getting all that 'crap' sorted out started my stomach acids to churning now and again. I came darn near loosing my Fundamentalist religion before getting the bridle on the wild horse.

I am not exactly a "Bible Thumper" but I do want to tell y'all about our little town's Presbyterian Church. They raked in enough dough (or is it doe?) to build a "brand new" sanctuary. They probably saved a "bundle" on account of taking out the beautiful stained glass of the old meeting house to use in the new one.

I think they will be keeping the old building, and I must say it "done the community proud" being a very old build having the style reserved for places of worship of that day when built. Even though next to our church I have never been in the Presbyterian Church. Just bet it has "plush carpet" on account I am told that is where the "movers and shakers" tie up their buggies at on Sunday.

Gasoline is well under a couple bucks per U.S. gallon here in this neck of the woods. We had company from Oklahoma over the weekend and were told it was down to a buck and six-bits there where they "take victuals and herbs."

Well today is "my rainy" day here at Wandaland where the cows are always hungry and I have nothing set aside for such a day. There is no such thing as keeping your gun powder dry on a day like today outside the bunk house. So, I am thinking on changing out all the stuff in the kitchen cabinets to different compartments just to keep Wanda surprised. She likes surprises, don't ye know, like a handful of roses now and again. In just a few days it will be seven (a perfect number) years since that woman done took out papers on me, roped me in and cut off my circulation. I guess it is time to start "feeling her out" if we will be celebrating this year at the BK or the twin arches with a bowl of Black Walnut "Blue Bell."

Oh, that kind of reminds me, I sort of over done it a bit this year getting all the stuff for building the Christmas Fruit Cakes. (By the way they are already on soak with whiskey.)

I have about a half case of 16 oz Black Walnut flavoring I would like to get rid of. Will let it go for $10 a bottle. This was another big month for Wanda, as she turned thirty-nine, ninety-five plus shipping and handling this past week and the folks in church sang "happy birthday" to her. It was actually a few day before and we went to this place where it aint proper to lick the knife or be picking a winner from the nose when wondering which tool to eat with. Ok, that's a wrap-up with news from Wandaland where the cows are always hungry and never milked, so I am riding on out of here. kp

Solicitations

Texas has a "don]t call me" law of sorts, and there are so many "loop holes" and exceptions it only deters the worse kind of solicitations. Hello folks, you have mail from way over here at Wandaland where the cows are always hungry, never get milking, and the only sweet stuff allowed in the kitchen come in those little blue packets. Think that was one of the pre nuptial things.

However, often times there are companies "out there" who appear to ignore the do not call list as it is perhaps more profitable to do so even with being fined occasionally. I imagine they can be reported to some place which is supposed to be "riding herd" over it. It is my belief most of the solicitors have a quota and may even have a time limit for each call. Probably most people doing the calling are those not qualified or unable to obtain other honorable work, and need employment. Course occasionally one of those professional "slick willies" who couldn't make it selling "time share resorts" has your number on their list. If I am not watching one of my favorite shows on the RFD-TV channel, it is mostly that kind I like to "mess" with their mind, and scatter their marbles, but sometime some others solicitors as well.

The idea is to keep solicitors on the phone as long as possible pretending to be a bit senile, ignorant and just plain stupid causing them to wish they had not called. Some, after five or ten minute will just hang up on you. There was once this guy who was so "put out" with me he said "old man you are ignorant." I told him "yeah I know, people tell me stuff like that all the time." I guess I got a bit too serious with him when I said "I hear tell it takes one to know one, because he hung up on me.

My strategy is to take control of the conversation, and say wearied things as if nothing much they say registers. One of my favorite statement is "I am so glad you called because I get a little lonely now days as hardly anyone calls anymore since my woman done put me on the don't call list. She doesn't like it too much for me to be taking with women folks. Do you ever get lonesome?" Once I told this dude my wife told me not to talk to telemarketers, and asked if he was one." As I said some of these people are not rookies, and will attempt to stay in control. His reply was "no, I am just making a courtesy call." My usual replies to those kinds of statements are "thank you for thinking of me."

Some telemarketers have tuff skin. I declare they must have sold Tupperware or vacuum cleaners door to door; having doors slammed in their faces, spit on and dogs turned loose on them, but was never once insulted. Sometime there are those who sort of loose control and get a little "smart mouth." I recall once telling this dude my wife wanted me to get her pregnant and I need to attend to it before she changed her mind. He took the bait and ran with it. He couldn't resist asking if I was still able to do that. I told him "couldn't say for sure but it would be fun trying." I believe it was this one who told me "you act like a card packing idiot, and wanting to have the last word hung up on me.

My guess is if a telemarketer scores one in a hundred it is a paying proposition, and they know many people will hang up on them immediately. Now if you are truly feeling your oats and want to blow their mind just give indications as if you are some what interested and ask a lot of questions about the product. When they go for the kill, start backing down and eventually tell them they will have to call back when the spouse is there because you are not allowed to make decisions on your own.

It was just a few days past, the next day after having a phone installed in my room at the skilled health center a "sweet sexy sounding" female called me and stated she was calling for the Tyler Telegraph. Now the Tyler Telegraph is the Tyler Morning Telegraph news paper. You can just imagine all the conversation which took place. I told her since the advent of internet I figured people sending telegraph messages was about 'tuckered out." I was then informed the Telegraph is the Tyler Newspaper. She said she was calling to verify the address where the paper is to be sent. I thanked her for the Newspaper wanting to send me the paper, but also said if it didn't have a lot of pictures it wouldn't get looking at much. She wanted to know if I was interested in knowing all the local news. I said nope, not what the media now days give out as news. She wanted to know why not. My response to that was because 98 percent is depressing, and people are going to let you know all the important stuff anyway.

There was once, and still may be a certain TV station which would commence their so called news segment with "Proud of East Texas" and follow that with a lot of reports of robbery, rape, stealing and murders. That kind of stuff is not news, it is just the same old stuff often times happing with the same people.

During the course of the conversation with the sales person I came to realize she was just calling numbers. In what was supposed to be an unsuspecting way it was made known my name and address she did not have. I wasn't about to give it to her either, as it was apparent she did not understand what "no thank you" means. She had been programmed to emphasize the free subscription for a certain length of time and send the paper even if not wanted. So, there is apt to be sent "Telegraphs" to a Jose Gonzales at the prestigious zip code address of the skilled health center.

Solicitations

Groundhog Day has came and gone for the year 2007 with not so much "fan-fair" except for the town in Penn. It is a big deal thing there. The mayor and the hog will come out and have their pictures taken together. Folklore has it, the groundhog crawls out of a hole in the ground on February 2nd (this year) and if he/she/it sees their own shadow, back in the hole they go for another six weeks or so to take a long nap. Wonder what the mayor does. Then there is February 14th, ah yes Valentines Day, and what women is it who does not like getting a big box of chocolate candy? People now days give flowers, diamond and sexy underwear to their sweeties. Valentine sales will be in the billions. Recon there is a couple generations who don't know about Dog Patch and Sadie Hawkins Day and bidding on a picnic basket.

Well that is how it is at Wandaland, where the cows are always hungry, never gets milk and where ole Ziggy the cat is to lazy to move. kp

TELEMARKETER

Hello folks you have news from Wandaland where the cows are always hungry and they never are milked. This is my story about telemarketers and it is only when I am in the crapper about to finish up with the paper work that I do not love to get a call from telemarketing folks.

I really do enjoy "breaking in" the new kids. You know the drill, they commence with I am "so and so" and calling to tell you about "such and such." Course I can hear some sort of giggling and sniggering at me and when I am put on a speaker for others to hear me. Some are pretty good pros and I get to wake up a few brain cell too. I come back immediately with "I am so glad you called because my wife put us on the no call list, and I hardly ever get to speak with people much anymore. Then there are those who probably hasn't had much luck all day so they figure, great balls of fire, I might as well go ahead and have some fun with the dude as this day is shot already.

My intention is to keep them on the phone as longs as I can, and act interested enough at times to make them believe they can rope me in. Well, I tried this once after a rather long conversation saying to the dude, hold on a minute, my conduit is leaking on account of my bladder has shrunk. It was true and I was having fun like one of the Darrell boys who had just rode into town on a turnip truck. I dropped the phone, and made tracks to the crapper and when I got back the dude had hung up on me. (Well you can't win every time.) I once told a telemarketing person to call back later on account of I was having sex. The dude actually apologized for calling.

There is an old saying which goes something like this. Give a spunky hungry fish a lot of line and they will run with it every time. Something which seems to get "new comers to the scene" off balance is after them speaking fifty dozen words and pausing for some kind of feedback from you is to be silent until they say "are you there" and or what do you think? I say something like, I'm sorry but I was thinking about my cholesterol problem and guess I wasn't listening too good. There was this one guy who said I'll be dam, you don't want me to explain that all over do you? I apologized, and said I would stay focused if he would. I got just the "highlights".

If you can belch kind of loud once in a while it might sidetrack a telemarketer for a moment and cause a regrouping of their presentation. Course you might be asked if you are alright (like they really care). A good answer might be, not really, I think it is about to start coming out the other end too. A good way to end the call, if you have that opportunity is to say I would like to help you out but my plastic is maxed out, but I do want to thank you for calling me.

Not a lot of news from here this week from Wandaland where the cows are always hungry and they never get milked. I am like gone! kp

Brain in Depression

You have mail from Wandaland where the cows are always hungry and never get milked. There is a bit of nostalgic depression concerning the past while remembering with some reminiscing of "yester years." Driving along US175 a day or so ago caused me to remembering seeing an old faded large orange disk advertising Gulf gasoline where apparently a "filling station" once existed. Before my and your presence became known to the world gasoline was a "by-product" of kerosene and was burned. Then came along the "motorized carriage" and has advanced beyond imaginations. It brought about many changes that have affected our lives in so many different ways. Progress, be it seen for the better or worse, has a way of marching forward with time.

I remember being a child walking to John Whitakers store at Lilbert and buying a nickel's worth of "coal oil" for our kerosene lamps. Good Gulf gasoline cost about twelve cents a gallon but of course it had to be hand pumped to a large glass jar on top, which was marked in gallons, and gravity fed to the car's tank. Gone are the days when "service stations" were service stations. There were free road maps, and with a five buck fill up two attendants would light on the car like a couple flies on a fresh cow patty. The windshield was cleaned, fluid levels were checked, air in tires were toped off as need and most likely the floor board was cleaned before you were asked about how much gasoline was desired.

I recall going to my sister's house when they operated a dairy and there was "real butter" on the table. Call it what you may, believing in you product and supporting the industry which supported making your ends meet. Many years later I found myself in a similar situation. I was living in Alaska, working in the oil industry when the price of Alaskan Crude became 45 dollars a barrel. (This was after a number of years when I had embarked on a career of being "oil field trash.")

Eqpt Hauler North Sloap AK

Needless to say I was not much concerned about the cost of gasoline or a gallon of milk then. Things were a bit different the year I got married and was living in Chicago. Gasoline was 20 cents a gallon and many times it was necessary to rob the "piggy bank" to come up with a dollar of change to buy five gallons.

America had an alarm clock to go off a good many years ago which hardly did more that arouse us momentarily out of our comfort zones. OPEC put the "squeeze" on. There were bets gasoline would reach a dollar a gallon before year's end; we car pooled and purchased gasoline on a somewhat rationed biases. That too came to pass before a lot of stomach acids got churning; the crunch was elevated in an acceptable way and we were back to building motor homes, SUV and bigger and better roads to increase "road rage" with.

We have seen interstates highways, "mix masters", "high fives" and various other "progresses" to enhance our fast pace of "keeping up with the Jones." Not many months ago it was advocated to not purchase gasoline one day in hopes that supply and demand would affect the price.

What I heard then was what guarantee is there if I do that others will. Course my position was I would just fill up the day before. It is a foregone conclusion the largest inventory of gasoline exists in the tanks of vehicles in the country.

I don't watch the news on the tube much anymore on account of my brain is attempting to come out of depression. Did see however where many people have commenced to "tighten their belt" in various ways to revert back to a lifestyle unbecoming to the "American Way." One gal said she could no longer afford those seventy-five dollars fill ups and had commenced to purchase only the amount to satisfy the immediate need. Well not this dude! I spend a couple bucks each day going down and topping my tank off just to beat the daily price increase. (The way I see it, it doesn't cost more to keep a full tank than an empty one.) In about the year 2050 I will have "outsmarted" the capitalists.

I feel certain there is a solution to our present dilemma, as time has arrived for radical change. Let's forget about a sluggish economy for a couple days and maybe one of the candidates for the "high office" will include gasoline rationing as one of their promises. We have to exercise a lot of diplomacy with such as to not offend OPEC. If we would commence putting people in jail for not using mass transit or car-pooling, that should move a few thousand from behind the driver's seat each day. Of course airlines have the privilege of exercising "free enterprise." Government has no business of telling airline executives how much they can increase fares to guarantee their wages as well as others PERKS.

That would be sort of like congress passing a law where they could not give them selves raises, perks and limit terms so others could have a shot at the "good life." I have a suggestion for airlines who feel they need to increase their revenue. Install pay toilets on the plane with a twenty-five cent charge for the first two minutes. Also install toilet paper dispensers which would dispense one sheet for a dime, and if three sheets is required to finish the "paper work" then have a slot where three sheets is dispensed for each quarter.

The airlines could impose a fee; say fifty dollars, for neglect of fastening the seat belt. I hear tell our landlocked police give out citations for offenders in vehicles where there is no danger of falling out of the sky. I am told they only do this during the week until their quota has been met.

Postage stamps sky rocketed a penny a few days ago and I am wondering if the cost of gasoline had anything to do with it. Business which sends you bill payments and loads of "junk mail" had to endure 1/10 of 1 cent so I am told. I am not thinking we should put government in charge of running airlines, on account they would no doubt come up with the idea of reducing business class fares as a means of "shoring up" the lagging economy.

Before telling y'all to keep your powder dry and wind to your back I do want to mention our problem concerning gasoline, and gases which are punching holes in the ozone are being addressed. There is a thriving plant in operation which is taking the "gas" out of cow puckey and turning it into gasoline. They are leaving in the fertilizer contents to be recycled. If all our foreign and domestic problems are not solved by the year 2017, I will probably run for president as my age of 92 won't be a factor. I envision a utopia where we will all have our own "beam up" home stations when we desire to leave the house. World hunger will no longer be a concern as one super vitamin pill once a week will replace human needs. Just think, we will no longer be bothered with a smart box to change analogue transmitted signals to digital. So Dick Tracey, Wandaland where the cows are always hungry and never get milk is asking, what else is coming down the pike? That is all the news from these parts. kp

LONDON LEAVES ARE FALLING

London Leaves Are Falling

You have mail from Wandaland where the cows are always hungry and give no milk.

There has been lot of London Leaves slowly fallen to the ground since that day I sat in an enlisted men's club in Subic Bay, Philippians helping to make Milwaukee famous. I was on my way home returning back to reality from what seemed like a bad dream. I sat there that evening listening to a beautiful and talented Philippine girl who had long flowing black hair with a red rose in it sing a most beautiful song about a secrete love. The song told a story of how the secret love had turned into reality. Most of the places where I had been the past three years or so we didn't have beautiful songs and . . . . . girls. The so called "forgotten war" had ended, and I was being released from active duty. It wasn't very long afterwards I learned the song had put Doris Day on top of the charts. And then came along The Sattler Brothers doing a song which tells the story of why we can't go back home to the "good times" anymore.

These are songs relating to reality, one speaking with much joy and the other indicating a bit of sadness. Since our little trip to New Zealand I am often time reminded of something Cousin Diane grand daughter said, "Don't be sad it is over, but glad that it happened"

Diane's Garden in New Zealand

Course I am speaking of the "good times," but I am afraid the misery we will soon be facing, if not already, will be more than gloom and despair If there is but one thing we Americans know how to do well that would be to "ride a good horse into the ground." Well, I am no prophet or a voice of doom, and just perhaps there will be a way to return home from a "bad dream".

I don't know, maybe I have been much "hung up" on reality all of my life. Times were in last century when people climbed their ladders to the top and were proud of their accomplishments. We worked faithfully and had retirement to look forward to. Then politicians came along and said if you will make me your guardian (top hand), vote for me, I will send you on up to the top in an elevator.

Oh how people can be snookered. We believe there were such thing as a "free meal" so the elevator became overloaded and the cable finally snapped dropping the car quickly to the bottom. Make no mistake, the true "American Way" is "moving on up to the east side with a deluxe apartment in the sky" must needs be the old fashion way.

Many people seem to believe one political administration or another can inflate the balloon once again and get it soaring high, not seemingly taking into account what we have today is the product of some fifty years or more of over indulgence in good things. "We deserve it" has become a household word. I am afraid it is going to be a turbulent journey back to Bethel, if we ever get back. We must return back to Bethel, and most likely going back will have to be the old fashion way as well.

We have turned ourselves into a society of instantaneous quick fixes and I want it now. The masses are hurrying to have cancer, heart attacks, nervous breakdowns, and doing other things as perhaps a by-product of wandering off course. I sometimes stand in front of the microwave and urge it to hurry simply because of acquired impatience. We are bombarded daily with "you deserve it" Banks seems to force unbelievable credit upon the masses. The false economical effluent is like a house built on sand for stability instead of bedrock.

Our coin dollars, quarters and dines are no longer of much silver if any. Gold coins were taken out of circulation many decades ago. When our government needs more money for things as stimulus and entitlements, no problem the presses operates with the speed of lightning. Our deficit is much out of control and mind boggling to say the least. It has become as an untamed wild horse running aimless who no cowboy has been able to rope.

Another thing we have learned to do well is depend on the government gravy train to never become derailed, and complain loud when it does. It is the government's duty to provide the repair, while we never lend a hand. We see government as the quick fix to everything broken and never have we the people are in self-derailed. It is believed my many the more "horse puckey" slung against a wall, more is apt to stick. Before the "haves" became the "have not's" there were plenty of people who at no fault of their own, had not a "pot to piss in or a window to pour it out." Perhaps there is as some say a war going on for wealth.

It frightens me all the ways in which our nation's heritage has been allowed to slip away. What have we succumbed to? Normally addiction to various things has to "bottom out" before there is a climb back to daylight. It is "hard to swallow" just to hear a certain religious sect is provided with a room in a public school to pray to their "god" while Christians are buffeted in such consideration. Judges are not allowed to have the very "corner stone" of supreme law and justice posted on wall above heads in their court rooms. Military Chaplains are ordered to not pray "in the name" of Jesus in public to not offend other religions and are court-marshaled and discharged when they do not knuckle under. God forbid that we have dug the hole to deep to climb out! We do need change, but where is it needed the most? What kind of change may I ask"

Often times various animals can sense something is about to happen and become frightful. We feel the wind blow from different directions and look to the sky for signs of a storm brewing. One parting thought, will we still be a friend to Israel when the blow is over? A line is being drawn in the sands of time. The numbers are increasing among those who say "as for me and my house, I will serve a'ala (Al-lah)."

I see turbulent times as we continue to "navigate much uncharted waters" for the world, our country and here at Wandaland where the cows are always hungry and never gives up their milk. kp

Henley our Cook

Times when I was in the Navy has done struck me mind, and I don't know just why. Some of the stuff I had just as soon get lost in the mind, and some stuff I sort of enjoy it coming back now and again. Hello folks, here's Wandaland again from over here where the cows are always hungry, don't git milking, and where we are now on the kick of drinking green tea sweeten with pure clover honey made right here in these parts of the country.

Just wished I'd scratched done a few notes on stuff, so when I got to reck-co-lecting on them times so to have real good particulars on stuff, but you know how it is with sailors, their mind are on other stuff. There was this funny chubby sort of guy who was always grinning like a possum up a persimmon tree. He was short and always a joy just to be around and I do declare he joined the Navy to get sump'en to eat. That boy shore did luv that fried up Rabbit which done looked a lot like the right lower end of a gooney bird. And then there was Henley the cook, I gotta tell ye on.

Henley was an alright kind of person who came out to the chow line a lot and would brag on the "slop of day." Actually most of the crap was pretty good chow he cooked up. Sometime he would do the serving and offer us regular folks a double helping of stuff. I sort of looked forward to Fridays when we would have for breakfast Navy Beans, stewed prunes and corn bread; however the "shit on shingle" was fitting too.

Henley never got off the ship much because of being "restricted" as punishment by the captain for screwing-up on those rare occasions when he was turned loose on the public. I recall once he got off the ship, when ashore, found some wine somewhere on the beach, got a bit too saturated and found his way to the officers swimming pool on base. He had decided to go swimming "buck-necked" around midnight and the shore patrol caught him. Another thing I recall about Henley is the time we went to the big island of Hawaii and done saw that be hole in the ground belching up them hot lava stuff. We could walk up close and look right over in there and see the hot stuff churning away. Well I was standing there by the captain doing some looking when he, the captain, call Henley over and told him to look and tell him the truth if Texas had anything like that. Henley scratched his butt a time or two and said "captain we shore don't, and if these people would call the Dallas Fire Department they wouldn't be having one much longer either." Folks that really did happen and pretty much just the way I done told you.

Wanda and I done made the trip, and we are back from her ancestral land, when the Stokes and Tedders families left from to go to Oklahoma. It was over in Georgia, and that is where we drove around a lot, but first going by the way of Alabama to see Cousin Sam and his wife "Y-Me." That is her name and I don't know how to spell it, and I don't recon she ever said. We drove a lot in Georgia looking at places where General Sherman done messed up a bit.

We traveled pretty much the back roads; it was like riding a roller coaster. It was up and down hills and around "S-curves" so much I done plum nearly got sick. If it had not been for all them pretty tree leaves, and old mansion looking houses I might would have. My how them trees were pretty. Some had purple leaves, some gold, some yellow, prettier than all those colors in the Crayola box.

There in Georgia, the county of Jasper, the courthouse is very old, and I am talking really old and there is a "square" with a statue of some dude too. Inside the courthouse the floors are still plank, squeaks a bit, but polished up so good ye could slip on them. All the rooms are big and the doors wide and tall. I think it was build back in the 1800 and has never been replaced. There are old records which go back ump-teen years also. Wanda found all sorts or records on here ancestors in them books. I aint gone bore ye to much with all that stuff, but this one thing I gotta tell ye about. Her great, great granddad had died and there was an inventory of his possessions to be sold off. He was a wealthy old fart fur them times, but one of the amusing items on the list is a "cow bell" listed as being worth ten cents. Lots of other amusing things as well, 'cause the list took about five pages of a hugh ledger. All the places we went and looked for information, we found the people to be friendly and helpful beyond all expectations. We stopped the search at the Georgia National Archives there in Atlanta where we didn't find any information we had not found already down in the two counties. On the way back home, near Vicksburg Mississippi, we were running a bit low on petro, and I needed to drain my own radiator so I pulled in at this station, and guess what!! Gasoline was $1.97 9/10 a gallon, and that contributed to an almost perfect trip. I guess it would have been perfect if it had not been for that "ratty old" motel we hunkered down at in one of the little towns. It was only twenty-five bucks a night. The two beds had thin mattress which you could feel the springs through, and the old pillows were knottier than and old pine log. We didn't ask about a continental breakfasts, ice machines, or coffee or anything like that as I don't figure much they "cotton to" knowing about dat.

It was good to return back to Wandaland where the cows are always hungry and never get milked. Perhaps someday we may make another trip to see "Wanda's kissing cousins." So that is what has been on our minds lately. kp

Geese in Formation

By

Kodell Parker

It has got a lot colder here at Wandaland where the cows are always hungry and never need milking and where our hot chocolate is sweeten with those little packets of yellow stuff.

I did not get to see and hear geese this year flying over in a "V" formation. Wanda swears she heard and saw them, two formations together mind you, but they were not connected to make a "W". It seems with the cold weather the moon seems bigger and brighter and more stars can be seen in the sky as well. We have the heater going in the horse's watering trough to keep his water from freezing, and our faucets are wrapped, so I say "bring on the freezing weather. It got powerful cold last night, down in the 20's and just a few days ago it was near 90. There must be some truth in the old saying "you are either a fool or a new comer to the area if you try to predict the weather."

I can hear that old North Wind whistling around the corner of the house and it sort of makes me shiver a bit even here in our warm cozy house. Well, there are a couple cans of Wolf Brand Chili just waiting in the pantry for such an occasion. Maybe the cold weather will kill off some of the creepy crawler things such as Red Bug whose only purpose seem to be to torment people. Patches, our dog, has taken to sleeping in his house and he even allows Ziegler, the cat, to move in on cold nights and snooze along side him as well. I was just thinking, it would be good if educated people could get along together as well as our dumb dog and cat.

Now that winter has caused all the "London leaves to fall" and since the county finally got around to trimming the branches on the trees overhanging our road, we can now see a long way. I can see things our neighbor, the one I do not like so well, doing stuff. I suppose the few deer which used to hide along the side of the road; jumping out in front of passing cars will no longer have a hiding place. Wanda thinking the county commissioner owed her a favor. She was after him all summer and fall to cut tree branches and he finally got around to it. Our Mexican friends who has the large heard of strange looking goats, gray and white Burros, a bunch of ole speckled chickens and roosters at the end of the road is probably glad because people will be less apt of running over one or two a day.

It did snow here bit on Wednesday night, just a light dusting over a thin sheet of ice. Most all schools and government offices are closed due to the weather. Our quarter horse Fancy is quite frisky with all the cold weather. She likes to raise her tail up in the air and take off running, and she can slam on the brakes faster than a speeding loaded truck hearing about a "bandit" hiding just over the next hill. We were out a bit late last evening and while driving home we remembered in just a couple days it will be "Pearl Harbor Day." Not much talk about that now days, and I suppose it has as much to do with there are not many people around anymore when it happened. Times were when it was remember profusely, and I wonder if there was ever a remember the Alamo Day.

Tomorrow will be our twin sisters birthday, and the day after that my oldest daughter's birthday, so happy birthday Teresa Ann.

Life is really good now days, and there are not many mornings I do not just wake up and thank the Lord for another day, and for a good night's rest and sleep. And when we thank Him for our food we thank Him for all the many blessing of life and ask that He go with us through out the day. We know that He hears our prayers and answers them in ways which are best for us. I might add, most of the time it is in way unexpected and not asked for. You know, everyone should awake in the morning being excited about what God has in store for them that day.

One thing I am neglectful about, and quite ashamed of as well, is to include our service men and women in my prayers. Regardless of what one may think about wars and our present war, and why these people are in the military, these are the people separating themselves from families and friends guaranteeing the liberties we take for granted, and often time as if they are entitlements. Just maybe, all that wants to will be able to speak with their families this Christmas since they can't be at home. Estleen I suppose that you and Bobby have not forgotten about the army, Colorado and chocolate pie for Christmas Morning breakfast. Probably every person who has been in the military has experienced at on time another "there is no place like home for the holidays."

Pretty soon Christmas Day will be here. We will be opening presents and careful to save the bows and ribbon in a box to reuse again next year. Of little doubt, later on in the afternoon of Christmas Day there will be someone special to call simply because you just want to hear their voice. Bed time will come and we will place our heads on pillows thinking "it was a nice Christmas" even though Santa made a substitution on our "wish list" to him. There is always next year! Tim, when you put all my "loot' from the Christmas Party in the car for me you forgot to take out the jackets, so maybe I'll just put them back in the closet for another year. I think Wanda has already started to anticipate after Christmas sales. Says she is going to buy a few more Christmas lights and stuff. Just maybe I want have to follow her in the pick-up to bring the stuff back. Better yet, maybe she will make some excuse to go into town without me.

The kettle I put on the back burner of the stove to heat water in for some more hot chocolate is starting to make a noise like it is about to go into orbit. It is also about time to start thinking more seriously about those two cans of Wolf Brand Chili, the kind that has been too long since I have had a bowl full. 'Till next time that will be a wrap-up from Wandaland, the place where the cows are always hungry and never need milking and the cold weather makes cocoa and chili something worth cooking-up. kp

Necked as a Jay Bird

There were good intentions of going to the Baber shop and getting a shearing before going to have a valve replacement job, but just never did get around to it. Thursday is the day the in-house Baber and Beauty shop is open for business at the rehab, so there is no doubt about getting my money's worth.

Most of the time when I go for a hair cut at home the Barbara will snip around with a pair of scissors to give the impression he isn't charging too much for the amount of work. Guess he never thought about me looking on the floor to see what comes off. I guess it worth it because he pours on a lot of that good smelling "foo-foo" stuff which drives the women wild! Back in the old day, say some seventy years ago, I might get a little scrubbing behind the ears with hair cuts, but like so many other things that has went by the wayside. A good shearing make me feel as necked as a Jay Bird!

A day or so ago the in-house social worker came to my room with a bundle of papers and wanted to have a little talk. He said it was part of his duties to meet with new patients who are hauled in. First "rattle out of box", well after a few pleasantries, was "if you could be any place you would like to be just now, where would it be?'

Wanda & Kodell Ireland Vacation

I thought for a minute or so and almost said New Zealand, Ireland and Muleshoe, Texas. (Muleshoe is a real place out in West Texas) I guess my mind shifted back in gear 'cause I figured where this was headed and all about. I said "right here in this wonderful place!" With a bit of a puzzled look on his face he said "most people say home, and I am wondering about your answer, can you enlighten me a little?" Shore will, so I said, and found myself saying "so far the worse day here has been wonderful, it is like being on holiday, and all the meals are like a banquette." That brought about another "funny look", and he said "and", as if there were some explaining to do. I told him the only thing lacking here was an indoor heated swimming pool, there is nearly always instant room service but best of all it like a vacation the government is sending me on and picking up the tab.

He had more "crazy" survey questions, one of which was "what do you dislike the most here?" I told him that I would advocate doing away with those little orange packets of sweet stuff and replace it with the blue packets.

One or two other question I had to tell him that I did not give out that kind of information or that I would get back to him on it. He did not linger and left out shaking his head a bit. Hope he doesn't think I am a real nut, but will not be surprised if a "shrink" come in the next day or so. That should break boredom!

Well, wouldn't you know it, it wasn't long before the dude was back knocking on the door. He said there was an important question he had failed to ask. I said "let it rip, and we will see if I can field it." He wanted to know if there were any suggestions on how anything could be improved. Wow, I had wondered why something like that wasn't asked. I told him for starters I would knock out the wall between rooms and turn them into Suits. Install large screen TV with HBO and pay for view and put in wireless internet service. He wrote some more stuff down on the form, and I kind of think he wished he had faked an answer instead of asking.

I went on down to the Barber Shop to ask about my appointment time. It is located about mid way in a long hall. There must have been ten old wimmin (ladies) all lined up and a couple inside under driers. The barber lady said, I will come and get you when it is time, as I have no idea when it will be. These old ladies getting their "hair do" are probably one of the better things for them to look forward to. Actually I think there is a little competition of a romantic nature between some of then and a certain gentlemen.

I have experienced a miracle! There was a night when no plane crashed, no ice water brought to the room. No vampires swooping in to suck blood. Heard a "man of the cloth" once say if you are not in need of a miracle then you are not a candidate for one either. He didn't say anything it could be delayed in happening. It is about time to report to therapy, so until next time from Wandaland where the cows are always hungry, never gets milking, and Ziggy the cat won't chase a mouse, it's a wrap-up. kp

Halloween

It finally happened, I always "figured" it would some day. This morning as Wanda and I were having morning coffee, just sitting in bed carrying on one of our invigorating conversations of "Yep and Recon" it hit like one of those SUV's which looks like a big diesel drinking , road hogging, gravel slinging trucks coming at ye. I am talking about that "big college word" Wanda done sprung on me several weeks ago, which even my mind couldn't keep track of.

Well this morning, with no warning what so ever it just surfaced to the top. Just bet y'all have had weird things like this to happen to you too, such as trying to remember stuff. Not even sure I can pronounce it (the word) correctly, and it took several tries for this darn "smart-illicit" computer to figure out what I was trying to spell. When the computer finally got it, **"colloquial"** I "drug" out the old "Student Handbook" version of Webster's Dictionary to see if I could get a better handle on the word. It says stuff like "idioms", "belonging to conversation" and a lot more "crap" like that, so I don't know if I am any better off learning up on the word or not. I think what it mean is, it is a word which really "aint" a word some places but is a word someplace else. That don't make a lot of sense to me, but I guess folks who do a lot of conversing and stuff needs words like that to do "snow jobs" on each other. Like they say on RFD-TV, "I'm a farmer" (and goat roper), plain and simple."

Recall the time when you were a junior or intermediate adolescent, and at the end of October rolled around, and there was a Fall Festival at your school? It was Halloween time at your school! Hello Folks, this is Wandaland from over hear (here) where the cows are always hungry and never needs milking. We still sweeten our tea with that stuff which comes in little blue packets. Our "Ole Blue Tick Hound' carries on with the moon when no varmints show up at night, to chase away barking and stuff. Well, I wanted to bring to mind those "good old day" of how Halloween "used to be" celebrated and probably should be more.

Perhaps you lived far from your school and was required to ride a bus to the school Halloween Fall Festival night or what ever it was called. Anyway there was "bobbing for apples", fishing for a trinket, a cake walk and all sorts of games. I guess the favorite was the trip seat over water where you could "chunk" a ball and cause a teacher to fall down in and quickly crawling out shaking like a puppy dog or drowning rat. Quite probably, as Wanda would say, most nearly likely, the church you attended had a "Hay Ride" (with a couple of chaperones of course to control smooching), and there may have been a roast wieners and marshmallows, a haunted house to visit, and girls had pajama parties with sleep over. Course there was "trick or treat" night when you didn't have to be concerned about harm coming to children. If you happen to find a burning brown bag out on the porch when answering the door bell you dare not stomp on it to put out the fire, ha.

"Times were" times when there were just simple "home grown" masks and costumes. In the 1950's full costumes became available in stores. Merchants commenced to market all kinds of merchandise in the 50's to observe Halloween with. Next to Christmas Halloween has become the most profitable for shop keepers. Ever really "wonder" how it all came about? You have of little doubt heard some troubling origin things about Halloween, okay so what! Are you going to let it influence your way of life, stunt your growth or commence dipping snuff, or something? Hopefully not! (Okay to allow it to stop puffing those Camels and Unlucky Strikes).

Early Irish immigrants are given credit for introducing "Halloween Observance" in America. Its origin relates back with the Celtic people of Ireland. It was a day which celebrated the passing of the "light days" (months), and commencing of the "dark days", of which there was a pagan festival. (I suppose the passing of summer) It was just after the great potato famine when the many Irish Immigrants came to the USA, began to "congregate together" in celebration of the event. It is said that when missionaries came to Ireland they gave the pagan tradition a new meaning, however many Irish people there held on to the old pagan traditional ways of observance and they were brought to this country when they came over and settled here. (Some involved, well I won't go there!)

The start of Halloween (which may have been "light years ago" "All-hallow-even" or perhaps once "All Saints Day") here in America is strictly a secular, American culture day to have fun, giving out "fist full" of candy and other treats to little kids who makes you an offer of "trick or treat."

It is also a time of "make believe" ghosts and gobbling, of decorating pumpkins and turning on porch lights to let kids know you are expecting them. We like to Oooh and ah over their costumes. I think along about the last Thursday in October is when Ole Charlie Brown spends the night out by the Pumpkin Patch hoping to see the Great Pumpkin appear. That is one show I do not like to miss! Adults have commenced to have "dress-up" parties. (Slick Willie & Hillary faces doesn't sell well so I hear.)

When different early immigrants came to America, such as the English, they brought with them their own ways of observing Halloween. As time marched onward, the American Culture "took on" ways of each, and "cast away" some of the cultic ways each foreign culture brought forth. America is certainly "the melting pot" for the world, so to speak. Well I would like to 'pose adults and kids going back to some of the "old time way" of celebrating Halloween.

Halloween was a time when parents told the children of their heritage and other stories of meaning to keep alive. There were "scavenger hunts" held in houses. Some people hid various articles in a room and had a "hunt" similar to an indoor Easter Egg Hunt. You could organize your own neighborhood hay ride, or weenie roast, or have a scary movie to see (if you like that sort of thing,) Cakes were baked with various articles in them, e.g. a ring, which was supposed to mean "certain things." Getting the slice of cake with the ring in it was definitely a "sign" of romance ahead, but getting a small rag meant just the opposite. There were hugh marbles to be found in them too.

If you ever try this, warn people to be careful there are objects in the cake and to chew well before swallowing. This is not a game a small child should participate in.

In a number of town and cities, "trick or treat" has been abandond except for in a specific mall or other places in an effort to "crack down" on associated violence. Perhaps with the passing of time, increasing population, and rise in all kind of mischief, Halloween as it used to be, and still is in some places will "just go away." My take on the matter is, America lost its innocence before 9-11. (It commenced with the Ten Commandments being ordered from the halls of school.) Perhaps Halloween will be kept alive in ways which are yet to evolve, who can foretell what will happen? Only "The Shadow" knows!

Finally convinced Wanda her little water system (which she acts likes is her's) will keep alive and well without her "bossing", and she bought it hook, line and sinker. Well so I thought, as "time will tell!" It did "con" her into taking a couple days off for a long weekend of fun. First, I went over to see Tim, at his work, 'cause October 6 (last Friday) was his birthday. In just another year he will be kissing the "twenties good bye." Noticed he had a good looking cheesecake someone had given him, and a big balloon over in the corner of the office. He mentioned that two of his kids had been chosen in school to sing then National Anthem to open the Friday Night Football game. Tim came across as being a bit worried about their son Carson Shane not responding to therapy as expected.

We attended the wedding of Kyle, Estleen and Luea grandson in Nacogdoches last Saturday afternoon. It was a very beautiful and meaning ceremony which was held in a huge beautiful Episcopalian Church. It was near full on each side of the isle. As you would expect "they" were all "decked out" like going to the Queen's ball. It was so pretty, everything associated with the wedding. Having had attended Angelton Worship Services when visiting Ireland a couple times, I could recognize the ceremony as having "elements" of Angelton worship.

Sister Retha was visited Sunday Morning. Her and husband Pete used to visit us quite frequently before Pete passed away and she became disabled. She had her hair cut short and had lost a lot of weight, and just did not "look a lot" the way she used to look. She was not coherent most of the time, but did recognize me when I came in. Retha talked a lot, well just about continuously, about "things" from a long time ago. All of her "conversation" was positive and "upbeat", with only a negative comment about something occasionally. They were not complaints, infact much talk was about what a wonderful life she had in the years gone by. One thing which she said to me, which I will probably always remember, was "you be a good boy so we can see all the family in heaven." Many times she mentioned praying for all her brothers and sisters. It also became evident that she wanted and enjoyed company. All in all it was a good visit, and there was a long hug when a staff member came to the sitting room to take her to lunch. I recalled many things in the past, even the time when I was a very small child and Retha would "rock me to asleep" in an old rocking chairs out on the front porch at Lilbert.

I suppose that most everyone has heard of "kissing cousins", whatever that is supposed to mean. I visited a "hugging cousin" in Orange, Texas while on the trip. She is a very distant cousin, and into genealogy research of the Parker Family. We had corresponded some via computer and telephone which is how I came to know her. When we arrived she did "hang one" on me like a "long lost cousin" she had been looking for. I was told many, and I am talking many things concerning Parker Relatives, and was give a picture of a forefather several generations before me. There is a picture of three Parker Women relatives, who are very distant cousins.

Yes, Louise I did intend to write you and the rest of the gang all this stuff. Oh we got gasoline for $1.99 per gallon down in the Golden Triangle Area, and were told over in Houston it was much lower than that. Tim, most all of the new GM autos can have their speedometers changed between MPH and KPH. How to do this is in their operating manuals. Wanda sort of "screwed up" and got it changed when doing something else and that is why I had to drive 120 (on the dial) to keep people from pushing me down the motorway (interstate). For a while I thought I was on our FM road where everyone figures it was made to drive "crazy fast" on.

Heard on the "news" where the Longhorns beat the Sooners once again this year. Looking through the "American Profile" magazine paper insert came across a receipt for "Hunters Hearty Stew." It calls for venison or buffalo or elk. Recon this would "go over" like a tird in a punch bowl in Alaska as it doesn't mention Moose or Caribou! It don't mention nutting 'bout goat meat either! Recon this 'bout catches up on all the "going ons" here at Wandaland where the cows are always hungry and never needs milking, so later Brow. kp

The High School Year Book

Hello one and all, you have mail from Wandaland where the cows are always hungry and we never milk them

Digging through a cabinet that I sort of pile junk in, the stuff I don't want to throw away and stuff I just don't hardly know what to do with, I came across my 1949 High School year book. This was the year I graduated from high school and walked out of the commencement exercises, as it was called. It was then I came to the realization of not coming back there anymore. Whether we realize it or not, school constitutes a structured way of life. Finishing school is a day which can seem like "light years" away for a kid just entering high school. The day to graduate from high school is eagerly yearned for and, sometimes totally unprepared when it happens, as was my case.

I guess even to this day, the feeling which came over me is one hard to explain when I went to high school for the last time. There was bewilderment, having no clue what lay ahead. Many years later I was to experience the same feeling and wondered "what next". It happened once when getting out of the navy, and another time I don't like to speak about a lot. A few kids in my class had made plans to attend Stephen F. Austin Teacher College after finishing high school. Becoming a teacher was not my "cup of tea", and I had not an "inkling" one could attend and choose another profession. I had considered a "trade school" but that idea was dismissed and lost among the "cares of the day." I remember a recruiter once coming to the house and wanting me to enroll in a technical school which taught electronics. I had not the "foggiest" what electronics was about and, the best the recruiter could do was to say "pin ball machines" were electronics. Well I never "took to" playing pin ball machines a lot as it cost a nickel in those days. Many years later I was to get "bathed" in electronics and commence a life which embarked upon the "cutting edge" of so many of its aspects.

Well I picked up the year book, opened it and immediately knew why I had never attended any of the high school homecomings. I had considered a number of my class mates as "snobs" and I have never enjoyed being around snobbish people for more than three minutes at a time. In reality, as I look back on those days, I apparently displayed an attitude which bordered on being a bit snobbish as I kept to myself a lot. I did not have the ability to "mix and mingle, meet and greet", simply socializing a lot like many other classmate did.

I turned to the senior section and commence looking at while "studying the faces" of my class mates. I realized there was none that I hated and only a few I greatly disliked. I think there were more than I realized at the time that I actually liked, what ever that is supposed to mean.

Most of the people in the graduating class of 1949 from Cushing High, I have never seen after that day. Yes there has been a few, two boys to be exact, I did make an effort to "go see" once years afterwards.

I guess it just would not be proper to start mention names as I speak of this time. A number of the students I have learned "through the grape vine" are no longer living.

There was a time when I might "bump into" one in Cushing on a Saturday afternoon. For a while, going to Cushing and driving down its only business street just seemed like the thing to do when coming home for a week-end. (It's a bit strange how you want to leave and, how you are drawn back occasionally.)

As I looked at each senior student's face in the year book, some for a bit longer than other, I could not but help wonder about a lot of things. I guess the first thought was what did they think of me then and afterwards. Course I wondered if they had "made it big" or had made it at all. I knew a few had "turned out" quite well, that is with respect to social and economical standings.

There are a few classmates of my graduating class I think I would like to see once again. But then as I "ponder" on the "such likes", maybe it would be disappointing. We can not but help remembering things better than they were, or even worse. When you have good memories, why meddle with them? I don't know, perhaps it is that thing called "curiosity" which grabs hold and overpowers sometimes. One thing is for sure and that is my judgment about certain things was quite flawed then. As I looked at the girls I could not but help thinking some were "pretty" who I remembered as needed a "make over" and some were, well just girls. It is a bit strange what my thoughts were mostly about the boys. It wasn't about sports or other accomplishment but wondering if they are "balding" and have arthritis, if they have a good retirement, and "such likes." I only know of one girl and boy, maybe two, who got married to each other, and no they were not "shotgun" wedding either. I suppose it could be said they were high school "sweethearts" who knew "one thing" "coming down the pike" after graduating.

When looking through the sports section of the School Yearbook, I came upon a picture of me in a basketball uniform having a guard's pose. I was never a "jock", and never had a desire to be one either. I recalled why I went out for basket ball that last year in school. There were two reasons, first because I would not be required to have "study hall", as practice took place then. Secondly I could go to all the games, have a "bench warming seat" without having to pay to get in. There was actually a third reason as well. On days in which there was to be a game we got to eat early in the evening at school. We were allowed to eat all the chicken fried steak and mashed potatoes we wanted. I think our coach knew exactly all the reason why I had went out for basketball and as result of such I played only a few minute at games and it was only when we were considerable ahead of our opponents. It was said, and I suppose believed to some extent, if you played on the team, well you had a better chance of passing all your subjects. One of our best players on the "A" team (later called varsity) might could have fitted into such a category, Let me just put it this way; I did not "letter", and had no jacket for some girl to wear, ha.

There are pictures of faculty members, and of teachers for specific grades and subjects. Some I just stared at for longer periods of time while a number of thought ran through my mind. Needless to say I regret not having visited some of these teachers in later years and express in some way or another gratitude to them.

For the most part, our school teaches had exemplary lives and, used appropriate opportunities to teach more than "book learning." It was in high school, not in church, where I learned the "Lord's Prayer", learn to recite the "Ten Commandments" and the "23rd Chapter of Psalms." One teacher, which I dare not mention, once had me to stand in front of the class and tell a story I had read in a "funny book" about "Little Lu Lu" as I had been "caught" in study hall the day before reading it.

I guess "funny books" were the worse kind of "contraband" in school back then. By the way, it was suppose to be a book report, and I did get a "c-+" grade, which was passing, hoo-raah! High school boys were allowed to smoke at a designated location but I never smoked, but did chew tobacco sometimes.

Just have to mention the 11th and 10th graders and, that it was "taboo" to have friends in the 9th grade, but I did anyway. There were two girls in grades below me that at times I wanted to claim as "my girl." I do not know what to say except they were very pretty, charming to say the least, and more importantly seemed to have "liked" me. These, I wonder if they "married well" and never lost their delightful demeanors.

A high school year book, I hope you have one and take it out once in a while and "thumb" through it. Perhaps it will "jog" loose a memory or two stuck on the walls of your memory bank. Perhaps such memories will cause thoughts of "what might have been." I don't think a little thinking along this line is bad as long as we snap back to reality rather soon, and so it is with fancies at bit as well.

"What could have been?" Have you ever "wondered" about such? I suppose most people do from time to time on many different levels. Just who is this real person living inside our bodies and what if this "real person" had been given a different ethnic body, and lives in a foreign place? What could have been if this real person had been given a different gender body? I do not think these are "what could have been" things we should be giving thought about.

We are, what we are! Think I heard Flip Wilson utter that "piece of intellectual" thought. But, how did we get to be "what we are?" Much we had no control over. We could not help being born on a certain side of the tracks, or what name we were given, who our parent are or were. I suppose from birth our lives were beginning to be influenced or shaped to some degree by the culture and society we grew up in. There is a natural inclination to hang on to our roots even though we may not display such.

108

Somewhere between the pages of the Christian Bible there is a verse which states "as a person thinks with the heart, that is the person", or words which means about the same. (I just hope that isn't meant to be taken literally as I do not want to be like some of the thoughts I have!) Our thoughts probably do govern our actions many times and, define who we are so it would seem.

We get Dr. Leonard's Catalogue every month which is a piece of mail I look forward to receiving. It has some fifty pages of "stuff", much which appears to be just "gimmicks" one can order. There are as few as four ads to a max of nine ads on the pages. There are lots of things to look at and consider which can keep me busy for a week looking. A couple things in a particular catalogue caught my eye", one being a bottle of 120 anxiety pills for only $14.99. They are supposed to relieve panic and other kinds of stuff. I guess for some folks who panic several times a day that could be about a months' worth.

The other thing in the magazine was a "Watch Dog" door alarm. Now this is probably not what you may think. You hang the darn thing on your door knob and should someone try to open the door it will commence barking like a dog. I just might order two, one for the front and back doors.

Well folks this is the way it has been here at Wandaland where the cows are always hungry never ever gave up on drop of milk. kp

No Underwear for Birthday

Hello everyone, there is good news from Wandaland where the cows are always hungry and never gives us milk. First a note to family about my pending birthday;

78th Birthday

I have plenty of socks, underwear and Old Spice. Secondly go ahead and make plans for the 1st Saturday in December in Nacogdoches.

As Gabriel Heaters, a World War II correspondent would say some evening in the daily new over the radio "there is some good news today." And there is still good news occasionally. Gasoline in Fort Worth yesterday was selling for $2.74 a gallon. People were lined up at the pumps as if though rationing had just been lifted. I suppose in a way it had. Also this past week Kroger stores were selling milk $2.50 a gallon. I am wondering if this is a preview of things to come due to people not able to spend money as if it were going out of style. I have sometime said if I knew that I would be living this long I would have took a little better of my health back when. Now it is if I knew my pockets would have a hole in them I would have saved more for dry spells.

The long, long winding trail of political rhetoric is closing in fast. Perhaps at the end of the trail many fears will be relieved while others will have their anxieties strenghen. I guess until then most folks will be wondering what the New Year will usher in. This has been a most unusual year in a number of ways as affecting millions of people in various degrees. Course I do not have to tell you that unless you have just recovered from shock or from unconsciousness We have all had our parade rained on from a drizzle to a "frog strangling" rain.

Political rhetoric has used the "race, gender, religion" cards this year, as well as fear in ways as never before in accusations. There was also a time (at the on start) when it was said the race would be decided as young to older people's vote. My suspicious mind cause me to wonder if the present "financial situation" was not hurried up for political reasons, whew I sure hope I am wrong about people's motives

I think it was President Franklin Roosevelt who said "all we have to fear is fear itself" and President Kennedy who said "ask not what the country can do for you but what you can do for the country."

I think there is much truth in these two statements which these Presidents said, but we have failed to remember and act accordingly. Many things we are fearful of never come to pass. Life preservation is an undoable instinct and is ever sub-consciously present at all times. As someone has said "it is hard to drain the swamp with alligators nipping at the heels" and when people are desperate they react with that which is seemingly best for the person at the time.

I have a problem in that often I fail to pray never the less "thy will be done" on account of I want what I want. A bigger problem so it seem is accepting "God in his permissive will (not direct will) allows things to happen and He doesn't "clue" me in as to why. Well just like the song says "we don't need to understand, we need to hold his hand" and there is never a good reason to ask the reason why. I forget so often that it is not "all about me" but "all about Him." It is not just about faith, but who that faith is in.

May God ever cause us to be strengthened in love, peace, joy and wisdom for indeed we are a pitiful weak people in need. We here at Wandaland where the cows are always hungry and never get milked, say bye for now and keep your noses dry kp

CASTING PEBBLES IN THE WATER

A favorite play time was to toss a pebble in a still body of water and watch the ripple effect. At the time, being totally unaware that such play afforded a "hands on" scientific experience, many pebbles would be tossed in and the waves created were watched until their movement outward became dissipated in the very environment it consisted. At the epic center, ground zero if you please the little waves went out similar to a radio antenna radiating sounds in all directions. Just how far the Omni directional waves traveled usually was in proportion to the size of the pebble and force of speed entering the water.

There are other kinds of "ripple effect" in life which are generated in many unexpected ways. It usually doesn't take a large pebble in life to have a ripple effect commence and unlike in water, these life ripple effects seem to become reinforced with growth causing a wide radius within its environment before it dissipates.

The things we do and say today and choices made are highly likely to affect what we say and do tomorrow and tomorrow and tomorrow. I greatly like the signature my niece Doris Marie has on her emails. It says something to the effect she may not be able to control the winds but can adjust her sails. There is a saying about patience which I might just use as a signature to email which is "patients is the ability to idle the motor when you want to smoke the rubber.

I guess it is all about becoming emotional which all people experiences at some time or another. We "spin out" while smoking the rubber and loose control which more likely than not results in a "melt down." We can't change the past, because it is the past be it a healthy or unhealthy past. Too much dwelling on the past is oftentimes a large hindrance with moving forward. I have read a few of those "self-help" books and I wonder if the authors are saying this, but in a different way. What does the Bible havr to say on how to be successful and happy? The starter is to be happy with whom you are and a good start on that is giving of one's self with whatever you may have, not expecting any kind of return. It may be that a smile or a kind friendly word is all there is to give. All people have one thing in common and that is smile. As Loretta Lynn said of Crisco, it will do you proud every time." I suppose one reason younger people are hesitant to speak to elders first is simply because of age differences. On the other hand

I have found nearly all young folks will speak back with a smile on their faces and with much respect when spoken to first.

Folk, that is how it is with me and my "squeeze" here at Wandaland where the cows are always hungry and don't give up their milk. So until next time y'all stay sober on Sundays and make it on down to be hearing the parson man speaking Bible talk. kp

Sitting on Wally World's Bench

Hold on now, don't tap the delete button as this is mail from Wandaland where the cows are always hungry and don't give up their milk. My add, no won't go there its "potty."

A few days ago I decided to drive on over to Wal Marts to purchase a few none essential things. When I stop and think about it, it is mind boggling sometime just how many thing we seems to think we can not live another day without. Anyway when I got there, which was a bit late in the morning, all the parking places close to the front were taken. It was necessary to park quite a way from the front. Times were when I needed the exercise walking but not so much any more. When I got inside I was a bit tuckered out so I sat down on the bench which is primarily there for us older people while waiting for a motorized cart.

Our Wal Mart now has so many motored carts it is almost like going to the fair and riding those bumper cars. There is a camera pointed right at the bench where people sit, and I like to just sit there sometimes and flip my finger at the camera several times. The "meet and great person" won't usually let me sit there very long doing that. Oh yeah, they know me down at Wal Marts! Could also be this kind of behavior is what got me voted ff the active deacon "board" at the Baptist Church. About half of the congregation will still nod to me, and the collections guys always hold the plate in front of me until I drop something in, so maybe there is a chance of getting back on the board if I will cut it out, but y'all know, some habits are hard to break.

As I sat there at the front of the store just watching the people coming and going, I sort of got carried away just watch and observing them. Actually I was blown away when I saw this young mother with a little girl who had rings just under their lips, in their nose, navel, and one probably close to other none mentionable places. There was a tattoo on the small of the mother's back. I got to wondering if she ever gave any though to being a grandma someday. I guess it was this which caused me to think about my grandma Parker.

Grandma Parker was a "stately kind of lady"; yet a kind and gentle kind of person, and the only grandma I ever knew. There are a few things in life which are just the way they are. They are like marbles in the sack which God gives little boys at birth to play keeps with. One such marble is little boys love their grandmas. Grandmas think their little grandsons are the greatest things since store bought canned biscuits too.

Seems like I may have mentioned a or couple three things about Grandma Parker in my Reflections of the 1930. Grandma would come for a two week annual visit when she lived with Aunt Lena in Dallas. She usually came about the same time of the year, and we would start watching the mail box real close for the postal card which would say when she would be arriving. Grandma could write a three page letter on one of those cards and her writing wasn't all that good to start with. Many times it was just a "SWAG" when she would be arriving because no one could make out the date.

Aunt Callie and Aunt Molly took after grandma about writing penny post cards too. One day aunt Lena would drive up in the front yard with grandma, and many time with Aunt Callie and Molly as well. Naturally we younger kids would run to the car screaming out "they are here." Mama would come out of the house with her apron on being just as spry as an old Pea-cock flaunting her feathers to greet them.

When grandma and all the aunts drove up and stopped out front they would step out of the car and do a shake to straighten their dresses. They were probably wearing their 'Sunday best" to make a big impression. Aunt Callie always had a big ball of hair on the top and back of her head which must have taken twenty hair pins to hold it in place. Aunt Molly usually wore a little hat when she came and it too needed a bit of straightening. Come to think of it, they were old women with black hair. Go figure! Aunt Molly's hat was probably one bought to wear at someone's funeral because it had a little black veil.

After mama had greeted everyone it was the kid's turns. We had to line up so Aunt Callie, Molly and grandma could ooh and ah over how much we had grown the past year. We had to hug their necks and give them a kiss. It is said that Aunt Callie would sneak a quick look behind our ears to see if they had been scrubbed lately. All I know is that I didn't much take to the hugging and kissing stuff.

Aunt Callie dipped snuff and she like to keep a tiny twig brush to brush her teeth with the snuff. Aunt Molly dipped snuff too and she mixed hers with flour which caused some difficulty in spitting due to it making a paste in her mouth. Aunt Callie and Molly never stayed with us much when grandma came to visit. It just seems like grandma coming was the happiest time of the year. Well, except for Christmas or Easter Morning hunting for eggs, but it was right up there being a close second enjoyable time. Grandma loved to sit out on the front porch in a rocking chair and shell peas in her apron. She also liked to listen to the Lone Ranger on the radio with Ossed and me. She really did get a "kick" out of listening to Terry and the Pirates and Jack Armstrong, the All American Boy.

There was a sad time too. It commenced the day when someone drove out from Cushing with a telegram from Aunt Lena stating that grandma had lived out her life and passed away. I remember going down to the barn and crawling up in the hay loft and doing a lot of crying that day. I suppose we never think of good family traditions ending until they just do. When we look back to those times we would like to be able to say once again "grandma I love you" and see her smile once again.

Like many of my cyber-relatives and rowdy friends we are now the grandpas and grandmas who love to have our little ones sit in our laps and plant a wet kiss on our face. We don't mind at all when they ask us many questions so simple that we hardly know how to respond to their inquisitive minds. This past Thanksgiving Wanda and I spent it with her people. There were five generations who came to have Thanksgiving together, and there were two pretty little girls for granny Wanda to hold and play with. One of the real good things about Thanksgiving this year was it was at their house and not ours. Someone else will have to face a lot of turkey sandwiches this year and leftover potato salad.

Wanda mentiond that we had our university this year on Thanksgiving and that neither one of us remembered it. She mentioned that being married has been an exciting time and seemed to have been just a few weeks ago when she took out papers on me. I urged her to be a little more explicit, and she mentioned going to Alaska, Ireland, Branson and now New Zealand. One day we will go to the Grand Ole Opera, we will, we will. And I with the big head was thinking it was all about me.

There is a cousin on Wanda's mama's side of the family who lives in Alabama she wants to go see next year. The first Branson trip was our "honeymoon trip" which Renee had arranged for us. I asked Wanda while we were talking on the likes what ever happened to our sexual relations. After a moment or two of silence of thinking she said "I don't really know, we don't even get birthday cards from them anymore."

I discovered a new soft drink while on Thanksgiving holiday. It is Zero Carbs . Calorie free . Caffeine free, a drink made from naturally flavored Sparkling water named Cry'Sta'l Bay. OK so you have known about it for some time. Yep, it claims to be sweetened with that stuff which comes in the little yellow packets.

That is all the news for now from Wandaland where the cows are always hungry, never need milking and where we play croquet out on the front yard. Kp.

Lye Soap

Hello one and all, here I am again sending news from Wandaland where the cows are always hungry, never need milking, and where Patches greets guest with a friendly bark and a wagging tail. Back in the late 1930 Flatlanders, Hillbillies and Sharecroppers in general would sometime sing a song about Grandma's lye soap, especially on wash day. It said something about it being good for washing clothes, pots and pans, scrubbing the head, washing the face and just about all other things on the place. There was a line about it cleaning out your "innards" if you cared to take a bite. I just imagine it would do a number on you worse than swallowing a chaw of "Cotton Bowl Twist 'backer." I didn't particular care for Lye Soap as I had to stir it in the wash pot while it was being made. I also got my head scrubbed with it at the end of washday after the clothes were washed. Not so sure I was terrible taken with water and soap of any kind

We don't use lye soap any longer since WWII, the big one, and there may be laws "again" cooking off a batch of it. I haven't seen any of that P & G Bar Soap around in several Coon ages either. Now I did like that soap, but mostly because it had a marble stuck in it. Well, what I was fix-en to say, a few nights ago I got all scrubbed up good, put on my best overalls and went down to the Community Center where there was candidates speaking going on. The main reason for my meandering on down there was because of the victuals they were serving up. However there was a lady down there all dressed up prettier than a "poll cat" out hunting for a "lover." I am talking this gal was mightily well coordinated and I am thinking if she can do that for herself she shore can have my vote.

There isn't anything better than deep fried catfish, some "musical fruit", hush-up puppies, and sweet raw onions to set the mood listening to several "wind bags" make promises they can't possibly keep. It seems like these events are a bit more civilized now days, especially after 9-11. Someone had done put up a card board sign which said "no booing, cussing or spitting on the floor." There was a deputy sheriff there who aimed to see to it that the meeting remained hospitable.

As y'all probably know, there are three Gospels in the "Good Book" which are called synoptic. Synoptic is one of those college words which means they all are about the same stuff. Now the other gospel is supposed to have been written by a fellow named John, and he writes about different stuff. The last chapter of John's book seems pretty much like an appendix. It is as if he wants to say "hey guys, there is something about my buddy Peter I want to tell you before wrapping up." When you get "right down to it" the last chapter of John's gospel has a lot to do with going fishing, and hauling in a darn good "mess" to have a "cook-out" with too. It was more like here was sort of a Men's Fellowship Breakfast with Jesus being the keynote speaker, and baked fish was the main course. Actually, the fish was the only thing they had to eat and no one was bellyaching about the menu either.

Ole Peter just loved to fish, and he, with a few of his buddies went fishing while waiting on the others Disciples to gather in. (Today we get on the internet to kill a little time.) The fishing trip wasn't planned, and if it had been, well no telling what-all that bunch might have brought along to eat. Fishing was very good that night and the next morning they got their bellies full of fish. I didn't make out so well the other night at the "candidate speaking" as they were a bit cinchy with the grub, but quite liberal with the "b-s."

Tomorrow is the primary Election Day and there is going to be some looser and some winners. I think my kind of voting now days is as much voting a'gain some as well as fur a few others. It seems like the real winners are the newspapers and radio stations owners getting rich off of "mud slinging" ads. Another bunch of people who are getting rich off the public are lawyers. We have issues with some property, and we got this dude to the tune of a "few coins" to make issues go away and I think he is too good at it, no. It looks a bit like he might be getting "out lawyer-ed."

Wanda's shoulder is "coming along" quite well. We go to therapy three times a week and she is able to use it more each day. I am not so sure we will load up the car and head north to Tulsa this coming week-end as Wanda has therapy late Friday evening. Wanda's son and daughter-in-law came Friday night and stayed 'till late Sunday night. It is always a pleasure to have them come, and a real pleasure when they saddle up for home. I notice in our weekly paper the burn ban has been lifted here and I'm not so sure that is a good thing just yet. A county maintainer came down our road shifting the gravel from one side to the other. Most likely a lot of it went over in the ditches, ha. Our commissioner is "up" for reelection tomorrow. I had voted early, and even for him but I wasn't 'bout to let him know it.

Recon that is all I want to say for now, so I'll be gone now. In the meantime y'all slip on by here to Wandaland where the cows are always hungry and we don't milk them. kp

Friendly People

Most of the people who work at "Wally World" are good common folks just like you and me. Many are working their "tail off" there simply because they need the income, though small as it may be. They appear to not be lazy, will walk a mile to help you find something, and usually very friendly and will talk to you about "stuff." In "spite" of all of this, including the many riding carts, I do not like going there. But sometime you just have to, so it seems.

As we approached "Wally World" we notice the price of gasoline was quite low. With the card I think we paid a couple bucks and thirty-five cents. I pulled in at one of the empty spot there at the watering hole and Wanda got out and gave the car a drink as the tank mouth was on her side. She was so excited about the price that she forgot to replace the cap on the tank and close the outer lid. After moving away, and driving slowly along the front of the store, looking for a spot to land we notice a number of people pointing and waving to us. We thought they were a bit friendly, but later we learned what it was all about.

Getting old and forgetful is not exactly a bad thing. Course it would help if you could remember where you last put you false teeth when heading out to church Sunday morning, trying to make the early service. If you have a good place to stash the car keys, say like in the "miracle-wave" oven, you will always know where to look for them. Short memory can led to some awkward kinds of conversation with the woman of the house. When you sort of "get out of joint" with the woman and have to ask a few minutes later if you are not supposed to be p/o about something, that can be a little embarrassing The good thing is when she doesn't remember just then either. Course it comes back to her a few days later when you least expect it.

Well, before I forget, while at someplace or another I was told that gasoline cost is apt to drop to around $2 by Thanksgiving and, a huge deposit of oil was discovered off the coast of Louisiana, one larger than the reserve in Alaska. Sounds like a good rumor to get started anyway if not true. Pumping all that oil out of the earth causes me to wonder if the ground is not apt to collapse someday. I guess this could all be just a rumor so as to stop building the hybrid cars, don't you think maybe? We have big gaps in the yard and pasture such as to loose a walking cane (stick) in if you are not careful.

I got to wondering about Rhubarb Pie yesterday, mostly on how you put it together. It seems there is not much discussion on the matter as there are few to no variations. None of the women at church knows much about it. You just cut the stalks up and boil them until they are soft. You mix sugar or perhaps some kind of sweet fruit with it and make the pie. One old codger "heard" me asking about it and said you could make good wine out of it. I am not into all that recipe stuff, understanding a pinch of this and a dash of that. I just know dabs and squirts. I remember eating some Rhubarb Pie once and thought it "fitting." Not many people grow the stuff in this part of the civilized world.

The Pie which is sometimes constructed for a "barn raising" or "log rolling" is the Shepard's Pie. Guess y'all don't know much about barn raising and log rolling. Have no idea how Shepard's Pie got its name, but if you make it with hamburger meat instead of lamb's meat it might be called a number of things such as a "cottage pie" or some kind of casserole. I am told that if you use fish, salmon, tuna, or sardines, it would be called a fisherman's pie. I for one can't see wasting a can of good ole Sardines in a 'fisherman's pie." Just maybe Sheppard slaughter sheep and made it a long time ago. To me when I make it, it just sort of evolves into one gigantic meat pot pie. It is something which can "turns out" quite eatable, giving rise to have the second helping, if-en ye throw in the right proportions of stuff. My "hankering" got the best of me and I crafted one Sunday afternoon and since it turned out reasonable well I gone-a tell y'all how, leaving out my secrete ingrediances of course. Now it will be a bit from "scratch", but you modern would be chefs and cooks don't have to go that route.

My main ingrediances are about five or six medium size Irish potatoes, about one to one and half pound of good lean hamburger meat. A double handful of thawed out "frozen mixed veggies." A goodly amount of them shredded up cheddar cheeses, one medium size onion and, let's see what else? Oh yeah, if you happen to have some celery, maybe a couple sticks of them, and one of those small cans of mushrooms soup and a small can of beef vegetable soup. Recon that's about it except for a dab of this and a squirt of that stuff you happen to have

There are lots of very good cooks who are as unorganized, as a setting hen trying to cover all the eggs, with stuff scattered about here and there. Then there are those who are as organized as "Hogan's Heroes" who like to keep things put away and "washed up" along the way. I lean towards being one of Hogan's group. What ever floats your boat, flies your kite, while a Nicky so I say.

Get out the old iron skillet, a large size Corning Ware Casserole bowl, (the big sucker) about a four quart kettle, and the handy-dandy food chopper from where ever. I suppose the can opener is fixed to the wall, or maybe you have one of those modern one which stays in the drawer. All of you who wash up the casserole bowl when it's contents are devoured know it's a good idea to spray the inside real good with some of that spray stuff which come in a small can so it want be so hard to clean.

Peal yo-are spuds and cut them up in little bitty pieces so they will cook in less time. Go ahead and boil them in the kettle as if though they are going to be "cream potatoes" for lunch or dinner. When they git done, start squashing them up with one of those "crooked wire things" smashing tools. Forgot to say drain off all the water first! While they are still hot and you are smashing them, dump it a lot of them shredded cheddar cheese, the amount you have a fancy for. Course you will want to add a little salt and maybe even a little black or white pepper. Throw in a couple dabs of mayonnaise and stir in too. It won't hurt any to put in about ¼ stick of butter. You want to leave them a bit on the "sticky side". Then set aside the cheesy potatoes to be later used in the grand finality.

I guess the next thing is to chop the onions and celery in the chopper. Sort of brown these two things in yo-are favorite oil in the iron skillet. When you 'figure" this looks about right, start cooking the hamburger meat in with the onions and celery. Do not over cook the meat, just so all the pink is fairly well gone. It is here where most people put in one or two secrete ingrediance such as a table spoon of garlic powder, maybe some powdered onions, oregano and stuff like that. I guess it is all according to ones taste. Drain this meat real good and go ahead and dump it in the "bottom" of the casserole bowl, spreading it out evenly.

Now put the thawed mixed veggies in a mixing bowl, which I failed to mentions at the first. Open up the can of beef vegetable and the mushroom soups and mix it all together. Here once again is where some folks put in their secrete liquid ingrediances, perhaps a squirt or two of Woshister sauce, or some catsup. Some folks like to put in a can of tomato sauce or perhaps some of those diced tomatoes with peppers. Once ye git all the stuff in and mixed up plumb good, pour it in on the hamburger meat. Sort of spread this around over the meat a bit evenly, and then put the potatoes in on top. Quite frankly I like to smear a little butter on top and even sprinkle some more of them "finely shredded cheeses" on top too. You should have the over warmed up for about 275deg F. so now pop in 'u-are dish. Pie, Casserole, or whatever ye want-a call it, in the oven and cook for about 30 minutes. Do not put a lid on the bowl while cooking.

I suppose that all y'all can tell, I don't do a whole lot of this kind of cooking or telling. But "the check is in the mail" if ye did fairly well. When the family sits down to eat 'u-ur "masterpiece", they are gone-a think ye have been "slaving" in the kitchen for hours when it only took a few minutes. As Loretta would say "it will do you proud every time" especially when ye see them eyes light up and hear all the smacking going on over the victuals.

Think I once mentioned Teresa and David became grandma and grandpa again a month or so ago. This time it is a cute little boy. I went over to see and hold him the next day after sliding out, and his eyes were not opened so much yet. He looked surprising well for a "new kid on the block." His head was not pointed and neither was his face red and all wrinkled up and stuff. His little ole fingers were so tiny. Most kid when the pop out have a looking like Eisenhower of DeGaul one, but not this tyke. I am not even sure if he came here "squalling" and "bawling" either. The name he got "roped" with (bestowed upon) is Krystian Paul. The: "Kry" is from his daddy's name and Paul from his great grand on the Swofford's side.

Many of you may have became aware that Estleen's and Luea's son. Ted, or Teddy (officially James Luea) has a son named Kyle who is getting married next October, close to the front of the month, there in Nacogdoches I suppose. His bride to be is none other than Sarah Brooks. Well, I suppose this is all contingent on one or the other not getting "cold feet."

Guess that is all I want to say for now, so until next time keep the burs out from under the saddle and wedgies from the under pants. We here at Wandaland where the cows are always hungry and never needs milking got a smite of rain yesterday evening, Aint it good to be top side having a compass, sundial and the "good book" to read all them Proverbs? kp

John Whitaker Store at Lilbert

Hello one and all, you have mail from Wandaland where the cows are always hungry and never gives up their milk.

It is November 2005 with the days, months and years passing by faster than a weaver's shuttle. It seems as if it was only a week or so ago when we were a bit troubled by the coming advent of Y2K. That too did pass like many other things, and we are being troubled by other things as the twin towers, Katrina, the war in Iraq and gasoline to put in the car. There are other things I like to ponder on now that I have started to walk like Fred Sanford. One such thing began with a "V" Nickel I found out beside the road at the Ole Parker Place at Lilbert some seventy year ago.

"V" Nickel was about as scare as hen's teeth then, but not completely out of circulation. They, like the flint stone arrow heads, could be found occasionally. I believe the "V" Nickel was replaced by the Buffalo nickel. It has a picture of a Buffalo on the back with a picture of an Indian on the front. They were in circulation for a long, long time and some may still be for all I know.

I do not remember just how it was that I happened to find that "V" Nickel, but just that that I did. I ran to the house to show it to Mama. She took it and placed it on the fireplace mantel right at the end where her snuff box sat. The finding of the nickel commenced a time of warting her to let me go to Lilbert to John Whitaker's store to spend it. As I think back on things I've about concluded the anticipation of something is about as good as something happening. I remember dragging one of the old raw hide bottom chairs next to the fire place and standing in it several times to see if the nickel was still there. The nickel was always there and it prompted another round of nagging mama to let me and Ossed walk to John Whitaker's store to spend it.

When you had a whole nickel to spend and a few days to plan on just how you will spend it, a lot of different things were considered. Well that is if it is about buying some kind of candy. Big pieces of Double Bubble chewing gum were a "copper" a piece. Sometime, depending on how Mr. Whitaker felt he might give you an extra piece. Then there were those big peanut patties that were as big as a saucer and so thick and hard a kid had a hard time biting off a bite. Just thinking about those cold RC Colas all iced down in the soda-water box (that kids were not allowed to keep open too long) is enough to cause one to wonder if something wasn't done to change the taste now days. After a lot of considering and looking in the candy case we usually settled on those long cameral suckers that were a penny each. I don't think that we were ever rushed to make a decision on what to buy. Perhaps one reason for that Mr. Whitaker seldom ever had two customers at one time. He probably never had more than one or two a day.

I don't remember John Whitaker's store ever having bananas, apples or oranges. He did buy eggs and I do remember the candy case being right up front on the left hand side. There was a small hill just before getting to the store, and as I walked up the hill the excitement of deciding on what to buy would commence to build. I don't know, maybe it was something that kids learned from parents in those days, but we shopped wisely with our nickels. Sometime it would be a couple pieces of bubble gum and three suckers.

John Whitaker's store often comes to mind now and again. When it was quite hot weather with little breeze blowing from no where John would sit out on the porch on a cane bottom store bought straight back chair. Maybe it was mostly because he dipped Levi Garrett snuff and didn't want to spit on the floor. John always wore wide black suspenders. I remember the porch floor would squeak a bit and a hole in the screen door would let a few flies in. He kept a fly swatter there on the counter to swat them with though.

John did keep the cheese covered with a cloth to keep the flies off it, and that was good. Don't remember buying much cheese there. That just wasn't something to spend a nickel on! The store had to be small, but to me then it was big. In the back was where he had a few dry-goods as overalls and high top shoes. High up on the top shelf were a box or two of Post Toastiest and Wheaties. Course there was a shelf for glasses and bottles of Levi Garret snuff, Prince Albert smoking tobacco and a few plugs of Brown Mule chewing tobacco. Sometime, most likely in the spring time, there would be a sack of seed Irish Potatoes, a wash tub or two and a horse collar hanging on the wall. There was a big orange Gulf sign on the side of the building. It was advertising the Gulf gasoline which sold for 12 cents a gallon. There weren't many cars in our part of the county then. He had one pump as there was only one grade of gasoline he sold.

Gasoline was hand pumped to a large glass jar on top which was marked off in gallons. It then gravity flowed to gas tanks of cars. I remember that gasoline was twelve cents a gallon then, and a gallon of coal-oil (kerosene) was a nickel a gallon. I suspect that John sold as much coal oil as he did gasoline. John kept a few different sizes of socks and women's handkerchiefs in another glass case next to the candy case. John Whitaker did sell on the credit and he kept track of people's purchases in a large ledger. I can't say that we ever bought on the credit from him or anyone else. Daddy seemed to think the "Good Book" was against credit buying. We just "made do" until our situation changed.

Walking to John Whitaker's store was about a three mile trek from our place and it could be an adventure within its self. There were a lot of little rocks in the road to kick along the way. Sometime there would be a rabbit or a bird to chunk a rock at. There weren't many airplanes in those days either, and if one came over while walking to the store I would hide under a tree until it passed. Then Noland Whitaker and Old Man Scroggins had dogs that like to chase kids and hurry them along down the road. We could hardly ever slip by those dogs even though we kept quite and tried. There were Persimmon trees on the side of the road which we like to eat when they got ripe, and there would be berries to pick and eat sometime too.

Daddy sometime went to John Whitaker's store. It was probably to buy a tin of snuff and just to catch up on community happening as he would be away for months at a time. Daddy had stripped carpenter overalls and they usually had a few nails and a nickel and dime or two in them. Sometime we got to keep some of the change to spend at John Whitaker's store. Daddy would let us walk with him to the store and we didn't have to worry about dogs chasing us then

John's son-in-law, Arthur Denny ran the store for many years after Mr. Whitaker died. I suppose the closing of the store was the results of Mr. Denny's death also. I do remember the old store building being vacant for some time, and then it got rebuild almost in the very same location. It too finally became boarded up with weed growing about it signifying another era had passed on, leaving memories of a past worthy of being pondered. No more news from Wandaland where the cow are hungry and does not give up their milk. kp.

Columbian Bean Man

Greeting to one and all, you have mail from Wandaland where the cows are always hungry and they don't give up their milk.

There are those here abouts who enjoy spending their leisure time multi-tasking on the throne with a magazine before the sun starts peeking through the cracks. No sir, not me! I gave up reading a year or so ago fur just thinking on stuff. My wee morning hours commences with feet planted on the floor and following that wonderful aroma drifting in the bedroom from its source.

Why it was just this morning I found my 2006 Christmas Mug, the one which still has a handle and no chips to booger my lips, right there beside a fresh brewed pot of "leaded" coffee. The favorite cup cleans up reasonably well in the washing machine now and again too.

My conduit to the outside world don't have an urgent need to visit the "facility" (d can, John . crapper) early so off to the big easy chair for some deep thoughts as the aroma makes its way up the nostrils opening the sinus.

Thought I'd get a jump start for lot of stuff while the eyes are opening. As I was slurping down a gulp or two of "Joe" I got to wondering about the Columbian Peasant working his way down a mountain trail leading a donkey loaded down with green coffee beans. Say, do you recall the ad on TV with the Percolator perking the musical ditty? Let's go back a few years more to the laundry detergent "Rinso" and its happy little wash day song. There was "Alka" with a fizz, oh what a relief it is. Where's d beef? My favorite was "come ride with me Lucile." That white over green 55 Holiday Oldsmobile had all the bells and whistles for it day.

Latest Scam, so I hear is that people are receiving calls from a foreign country stating that there is a problem with their bank account and they should give their correct bank account number and pin to clear the matter. Lot of "moo-low" is getting out of the ATM's over the net somehow. Then there is the worm, Trojan, whatever, what is suppose to "blow" the PC's mind if you open an attachment of #1 enemy being strung up.

I wonder what it was that caused Clyde Crashcuff & Leonardo to stop inventing stuff like electricity on TV Saturday mornings. It may have something to do with ratings or they ran plain out of stuff to invent.

They had billions of those electrons bouncing from one atom to another and once (for mature audience eyes and ears) there was one gay electron what done tripped a circuit breaker. kp

Sugar Daddy

If you happen to have, and can locate it, one of those authorized King James Bible, it can be read on some of those thin pages about two cities, one named Sodom and the other Gomorra. Sometimes a preacher will make reference to these cities when speaking on certain sex subjects.

Just a day or so ago, me and the woman of the house, was having victuals (pizza cuisine) at a certain place she like to belly-up to the table at. While having a slice of that wonderful chow in came a couple which caught most everyone's eye.

The female was wearing a tight slip over shirt which accented the super-sized "hooters" attached to her chest. Across the front of the shirt, where you would expect was written in beautiful pink coloring "daddy's sugar" or was it "sugar daddy?" Course this female was escorted by "Viagra Man."

Guess we could have pizza brought in (delivered) but there might be a gasoline surcharge. Saw on the news where Dallas is considering a fuel speeding ticket surcharge. Who and for what next will someone jump on the band wagon? I say these surcharges should be sent to the government. Don't recon the ambulance people can charge extra for hauling me in on account of I have six more months on my prepaid contract with them. Maybe the fire department will follow suit.

I aint done a whole lot of worrying on gasoline prices but I am about bread going for five bucks a loaf. I plan on getting me a mule to ride and I shore wont be getting no speeding ticket for that. I wrote the "donkey headquarters" that seem to know about all stuff asking what are speed laws on farm roads for mules. Recon they are planning on getting back to me on that, but I was informed I shouldn't be using gasoline that crude oil had to be drilled for. They said I could get a real good deal on an electric mower almost fur nutting. I recon they never heard of it taking fossil fuel to make them electricity. Beside all that I got several mowing machines out in the pasture, I am talking the 4-leg kind that only pollutes the pasture and not pretty sandy beaches.

It was back in 49 when my Pappy said if snuff went up to two-bits a tin it would still be worth it. I recon some folks here and about think on gasoline in the same way, that is worth the cost. I did notice the price drop a little. I got it for 1/10 a cent per gallon less yesterday. I save two cent and that is significant on account I can call people in far away places for 2 cents.

It wasn't like I was breaking a New Years' Resolution or the such like when I went back watching some of them "spend doctors'" on the tube. One of them gals spoke a good 10 words per second with gusts up to 20 when she got all wound up and someone else tried to horn in.

Like I have always said, all the important stuff ye can hear at the pool hall or Joe's Crab Shack. I hear tell one of my favorite programs back during the dark ages, Get Smart, Maxwell that is and agent 99 will have a movie out soon. Agent 99 was right up there with Wonder Woman and Zena princess warrior.

It is still as hot here as blue blazes and those tormenting red bugs ye can't see are ganging up to do people miseries. I got one on me and have took to scratching which makes Patches the Ole Blue Tick hound look pale in contrast.

Ms Ella I save the pics of you guys hoofing it off to Russia for the games. Believe it or not we saw just a little of a game here in the colonies. I think your team was playing. Never heard how it all came out.

I got me a good eye exam today in Tyler, and there was none of this "sees better one or two." Comes 'morrow I'm gone-a find myself down at Wally World looking for some designer frames; get some mail order spectacles, but just one pair just in case I got 'hood-winked gain."

Since my tank done run empty its time to saddle up and ride on out. Till next time from Wandaland, where the cows are always hungry and never get siphoned, y'all keep your powder dry and keep drinking green tea. kp

Cajun Coffee

Here is your weekly News from Wandaland where the cows are always hungry and never get miked.

This morning as I was sitting at the breakfast table lingering over the last bit of coffee in my cup I could not but help noticing it is past due to have a hand soap and water scrubbing performed on the inside of this special cup daughter Teresa gave me several year ago. Running it through the dish washer would be about like running the car through one of those $1 car wash. This time it will most likely take something a little stronger than soap, like a few days soaking with some bleach to get all the stain out. I just like for my cup to stay "seasoned" that way. Eventually Wanda will say after it becomes heavy "that's long enough, it's had it." Well the coffee won't taste the same for a few day.

Back in the days when I live in a little north of Houma, Louisiana in Terrebonne Parish we had a full fledged bred and born Cajun neighbor who I sometime would go and visit for a spell. That has been so long ago that I do not even remember his first name or our street name there either, but I sure remember his coffee. His "family" or "sir" name I can still remember but can not spell. Not ever wanting to insult him when I visited, I never refused to drink coffee. His pot was a small porcelain sock filter drip kind which never held more than five or six of those extremely small cups, and was more chicory than coffee. It was pretty hard to "down the hatch" with just one small cup, but I never refused the first "go around" or one a bit later on either. The third cup, now that's a different story! These Cajun people's cups would not hold more that two or three good swallows, but you were just supposed to sip it. It was always sweetend in the pot as it was making and usually had an egg shell in it as well.

Back in my Louisiana days, especially around Morgan City, we "normal talking people" were always asked if we wanted "Texas Coffee" or "Louisiana Coffee." Morgan City is along the Atchafalaya River and just across from Berwick. These towns were shrimp fishing little towns until drilling for oil commenced out in the gulf. There once was a time when a shrimp boat was parked right in the divided road way as you entered Morgan City from the river side. Those crawfish and crab boils on Friday nights over on the Berwick side down beside the river was quite an adventure. It was a place where I liked to "pig out" like one of the locals. Well, there are coffee drinkers and connoisseur of coffee, as well as crawfish eaters and I'm not much of either. We once had a coffee connoisseur boat skipper who could tell within ten minutes or so when coffee was made.

In looking at all the pictures Johnny took at the Christmas Party I see that mine has me with my RFD-TV cap on. I like to were it just about everywhere now days and would ware it to church if people wouldn't think me to be stupid and yank it off my head or something.

It is okay for women and little girls to were their hats inside in church and I wonder why men can't wear their caps inside. Guess someone would wear a "Coors Beer" logo cap and that wouldn't be to appropriate so that's why men's caps are prohibited. Like one of the Polka songs says "there is no beer in heaven and that is why we drink it here."

Actually I think I know the real reason for no men's hats or caps. That would be because of some religious teaching with a beginning in centuries past. I suppose men not wearing dress hats today it is as much a culture thing as any thing else. Not a lot of men wear dress hats and three piece suits anymore to churches, funerals or other places. Anyway I like my denim RFD-TV (rural American's most important network) cap. It came with a year's subscription of the magazine. RFD-TV is a pretty good TV station to settle in with on a Saturday night with a sack of popcorn as it has a lot of country shows. The Midwest Country show from the little town of Sandstone, Minnesota is especially good. Sometimes "Pop Goes The Country" is good when it doesn't have a whole lot of "Pop" singers. My November-December magazine was on the coffee table unopened until the new one came a day or so ago. I just wanted the cap to were.

Amidst all the arm load of newspapers, letters from credit card companies offering us credit just for the asking which come in the mail several times each week there are some interesting "junk mail" kind of magazines. I wonder just how all these people know our address here at Wandaland. It is kind of scary thinking people know more about me than I can remember about myself sometimes. Actually I have never forgotten where I live, but there have been times when I could not remember our home telephone number. I guess that is because I've never have occasions to call home much. One of the magazine came advertising several different "cuts" of steak which can be sent from Ohio. They look real good in the magazine but they cost a "bundle" for only a few 6 to 8 ounce stakes. There are all kinds of other interesting foods in the magazine as well, but I think I'll just keep buying steaks from the butcher shop. Maybe I'll do some ordering someday when going to town will become a real chore. I don't read magazines and newspapers much anymore, or watch the so called news on the tube a lot either. People tell me all the important things I need to know anyway, and I don't have to listen to something being repeated fifty times or more. It seems that often time these TV people just try to "manufacture" something to keep "jaw-jacking" just to take up time. I did hear however on TV that over in London, England they have phased out those "two story" city buses. Wow, I was glad to learn that! I might go to the Mother Land one day and need a ride.

When I crank up the computer and the home page finally comes up I'm hardly ever curious enough to look at all the advertisement on it. I just go on to my mail or my book mark places or whatever. Occasionally I will take time out and just look at all the advertisements on the home page, but don't click on all the individual stuff, as that would take weeks. There is a little section which lets me know how cold it is outside, and another one for the national news highlights. I once had a section which indicated what some stock was worth until it started to loose a lot. I didn't want to be reminded so much of that so I made that one go away. Once I scrolled on down and notice that Wal Mart had a link on it too. I decided to click on it and see what would come up.

Surprisingly enough to me one can see all their advertised sale items. Before I got to that part I had to put in my zip code and low and behold I was given the places where ten different stores are located within 50 miles. Well I got out of there as fast as I could being afraid that I might push the wrong button and have the computer start coming up on their page each time I turned it on or something.

My "squeeze" went to the doctor in Athens last Wednesday and got scheduled for a MRI later on next week as preparation study for a shoulder operation. We decided to drive on into Tyler and do some Christmas shopping after the appointment. Later on we went to Sweet Sues there on the loop and had dinner out which was very good. Their banana pudding makes a trip to Tyler very enjoyable.

It is getting on to that time when I need to put on some boots and go on out of here to feed the cows. Just maybe there won't be a lot of fresh cow patties for Patches to watch out for. Usually he is pretty good dog not stepping in them. He likes to go down with me and bark at the cows as they butt each other finding their feeding spot. Tomorrow will be the day to go and buy something for Wanda to take back the day after Christmas. People about seems to have gone "all out" decorating their places with lights this year. I just wonder if we in America really do realize how blessed we are.

Teresa we will try to come Christmas Eve. Until next time that's about it from here at Wandaland where the cows are always hungry and never need milking and where we sweeten our tea with those little packets of yellow stuff. Merry Christmas and Happy Trails everyone. kp

Forwarding e-mails

Hello to friends, hillbillies, hugging cousins and to any peers there may be left in their winter years from Wandaland where the cows are always hungry and have not a drop of milk to spare.

The internet is similar to other Media in that it has a great capacity to distribute all sorts of information, be it false or true, contain a little of each, and of recent or old origin. It has an advantage over most other media in that it's near instantaneous. Things such as e-mails and blogs have the ability to have information selectively delivered like a newspaper or magazine subscription would be.

Ordinarily when we read an article on a particular subject we should consider the author or "by line" before accepting what is written at face value. Even then they can be misleading intentionally or unintentionally. Often times there may be an undetected motive behind what has been written or said. This perhaps could not be truer than with television and radio news media with various "spin doctors."

This brings me to e-mails a person may receive or send, and especially to those that contains a "forward." I receive many e-mails each day with a great number being something forwarded, or containing an attachment which is being sent. I personally do not consider "forwards" sent to me by most people as an endorsement of the forward, unless the sender states in someway or another it is believed to be true. Even that may or may not influence what I think on the subject matter. Sometime someone who "forwards" something and is a bit suspicious of the validity of such will say something to that effect.

There is an "old saying" where there is smoke, there has been a fire. And this "old saying" is counteracted with "if there is a shred of evidence of untruth then the entire statement should be discounted."

I once had a dear close friend, who has since went to his reward, could not see anything except as "black or white." While I do not subscribe to the theory or "way of life" that the "ends justify the means", I have given a lot of thought to that proposition and have about concluded such is a proverb, meaning nearly always true, but not always. I do not believe "in wrong as a means to do well either." I do believe that sometime it is best to not divulge everything someone knows in certain circumstances.

Often times when we hear "situation ethics" we have a tendency to think in terms more as personal morals than standards, which are apt to be changeable by an individual, community or a society in given situations, but not to kind. Ethics is related to conduct and morals. I personally do not believe in all things being relative to something else. That is, I believe there are absolutes especially where God has spoken in saying we "shall" or "shall not."

So now I will "cut to the chase" and get on with my general sentiments as to why people send and receive e-mails which contain "forwards." Some e-mails contain jokes which the person sending probably thinks are funny, which could possibly be only is so to the sender. Some people send out recipies for various food "dishes" and may even say they are very delicious, but once again maybe not so for many people who receives the e-mail. (And don't we all just luv those email which contains picture on vacation with a note which say "wish you were here!' Yeah, I think not so!) You probably get the idea; things we forward are usually thing we are interested in or think perhaps others may be. Most e-mail received by me I do not have to ask "why are you sending this to me?" I would have to say most every time it is quite obvious WHY when the person it was received from make no reference to reason why. In a way they are similar to hearing speeches. We can usually determine if the speech is impromptu or prepared. Also we can usually determine if the speech is meant to be persuasive or informative. A course I took "many moon ago" in effective communications, be it oral or otherwise put forth the teaching the main reason for communicating in the first place is to place a mental picture in the minds of others. Think about it, we attempt to do this in many different ways, sometimes even successfully but many times to no avail.

In closing I will 'fess-up and say about News from Wandaland, usually most things mentioned have crossed my path in someway at sometimes. It is not unusual for the story to be embellished a wee bit here and there.

There is this story which is a little "potty mount" about hearing, and seeing things which are highly doubtful, and it goes something like this. There was a small mouse running to and fro in the room where a little girl about the age of twelve was at and she had the "womanly instinct" of being afraid of a little mouse. The little girl manages to get on a table in the room and watch the little mouse as it move about. Then suddenly the mouse hoped upon the table with the little girl, and wouldn't you know the little girl was wearing a pretty dress. Having no other hiding place the mouse ran up a leg of the little girl. The little girl thought the best thing to do then was to squeeze her legs together in an attempt to kill the mouse. So she did, and unbelievable she squeezed a pint of water from the tiny mouse; the object lesson to that story is perhaps things are not always as they seem to be. It is a proven fact the majority of people see and hear what they are prepared or desire to hear and see, to include many things which are not so.

Shadows are growing long here at Wandaland which means it is time to saddle up, ride on out to where the cows are always hungry and never get milked. Until next time wear a large brim hat and keep your powder, gun powder that is, dries 'till the next news from Wandaland. Want to mention my brother James is back at home after a valve job and a couple bypasses. It all took about four hours, was in ICU for about 24 hours and then in a regular room for a couple days. That is what I would say not "stick around" long enough to dislike the food and have a craving for a Big Mac

So until next time a northerly wind comes bringing mail from Wandaland where the cows are always hungry and don't give up their milk I'll say so long for now. kp

Thrilling Days of Yesteryear

Return with me now to those thrilling days of yesteryear when out of the past came the thundering hoof beats of the "Little Rascal Gang." Ah yes, the Lone Ranger, Terry and the Pirates and Jack Armstrong, the all American Boy. Mailing in three box tops of the cereal you just hated to eat would spring you a "decoder" for secrete messages. Kids had musel powered "cars" they made and didn't look much like a "Flint Stone" Jalopy. We had our sling short made with a forked tree limb, strip of rubber from an old inner tube, and the sling cradle from the tongue of an old worn out shoe. Competition was to see who could shinny up the tallest sapling tree, or knock a bird off a tree limb with the sling shot.

To be King of Road you need to have two front pockets bulging with marbles you had won in "keep" games. It helped if you could acquire a few of your friends' tops by knocking their tops out of the ring with yours. We wore holes in the hip pockets carrying yoyos around. We had our tree houses which was absolutely off limits to anyone (especially girl) who didn't know the secret pass word. We traded our "big little books", the ones about four inches square and two inches thick. There was some you could flip the pages fast and have your own movie. We rode our bicycles, sometime giving a buddy a lift on the handlebars, to our ole swimming hole. We played baseball out in the pasture on Sunday evenings after church against kids from other neighborhoods.

Somehow another we got through those "awkward years" as normal kids do, but me, uh hu not so much. Well I probably did do some silly things to make "Glynola" like me. There was the year she did not come back to school. I looked and looked and looked and finally decided she had gone away and it was going to be a year without a friend. If you were lucky you had a buddy who had wheels and could go cruising Saturday nights and have malt at the drive-in while girl watching. I guess the most memorable thing in high school did have to do with academic stuff. Old lady "so and so" who was my English Teacher and did referee in a study hall room I was in. She snooker in behind me as I was engrossed in reading a comic book and caught me reading. She gave me that evil eye look, and I thought until a few days after I had got away from it. Then one day, much unexpected I was called upon to stand before the class and do an oral "book report." I tried to beg off saying I had not finished reading a book yet, in which I was quickly corrected. I had to stand before the class and give a report on the Little Lu Lu comic book I was reading in the study hall. Guess what! I got laughed at a lot, but I made the cut.

I had to wait until grown and making kids of my own before I was ever in a "soap box" car Derby race. Maybe that (and a go-cart later) is what steered my son towards being an owner and driver of a race car for a year or so after he graduated up to a Big Mac. that is. He had to quit because of sponsorship, but he did win a race or two. He never "hit me up" to be a sponsor. Not so much happening in these here part especially at Wandaland where the cows are always hungry and we never milk them. Time to batten down the hatches so I am out of here. Kp

Replacing My Engine Valve

The odds are not greatly in favor of a patient who does "hard time" confinement for several week in a hospital of not becoming a bundle of nerves before being paroled. Not even an occasional four hour pass for trustees with good behavior is apt to prevent it, and could even have effects other than the intended. I suppose one reason for becoming a "basket case" while being imprisoned (hospitalized) is because of all the ongoing petty annoyances to dwell upon. Just where would we all be with no hope of a better tomorrow? We know there is coming a time when the insurance will stop paying and you get to take that last wheel chair trip to the front door. One of your worse fears, like a bad recurring dream, is of being lost in the system, and people thinking you are hanging out there because the food is so tasty.

Hello folks. This is Wandaland from way over here where the cows are always hungry and never gets milking. Yep, it will be very good to be home again, and I am most sure Patches, the Ole Blue Tick Hound, will think so as well. He likes to jump in the Pickup and ride with me around the place. Sometimes he forgets just who it is to ride "shot-gun", and get in the driver's seat.

Before getting "strung out" on this ordeal, allow me to first express my sincere appreciation to many people for their concern and prayers. Thank you for your praying for my devoted wonderful wife Wanda, for my surgeon and also me. Much appreciation for a number of friends and relatives who came to visit which changed long dreary days to pleasant ones. All the flower arrangements sent was very pretty. They, with the "get well wishes" (cards), and e-mails certainly help chased away a lot of gray skies. I am much reluctant to mentioned names for obvious reasons; however I do want to mention Amanda, a young granddaughter that brought me a big "get well" balloon. It floated about the room ceilings for a number of days before loosing helium, and her older sister brought me a beautiful guardian angel lest I should forget. There are those in far away lands which sent their best wishes with cards and e-mails, and oh what such a surprise. Need I say more except they brought much happiness. Thanks for being so thoughtful. There is much more rehab to take place before being "out of the woods" and purring like a well tuned machine.

My SWAG is that I will get approved to do driving of an automobile in about a week and will be able to be at home going to out-patient therapy a few days a week.

As alluded to, it is very hard to keep a positive attitude all the time when in a hospital. This is especially true when you are greatly out-number by others patient who feel worse than you, and surrounded by many whose discontentment seems to grow daily. Now when this little situation is mixed with staff people who seem to come to work after taking a hand-full of "bitter pills" before leaving home, there is little wonder of why little battles are underway all over the place at any given time. Before traveling on down this road I must admit many times "things" are not always as they seem to be.

Wow, can this ever be true when you are forced fed many pills every few hours of various sizes and colors making it feel is if thought your head got screwed back on a bit cross threaded. Where have all the cute little nurses gone off to anyway?

Three words which will not usually be heard spoken by staff people in hospitals are "I don't know!" These people are not a lot different in this respect from people in other "walks of life." When given the opportunity most humans are a little more than willing to impress others with their knowledge of their profession and other related matters. Now on the other hand, those whose responsibility it is for the train to move along the tracks smoothly, having only a few squeaks now and then, may often times be heard saying "this is the first I've heard of that."

After a day or two in intensive care you get bumped out of there to the first available bed to a place of less intensive care. I am thinking there are a number of reasons for this. (Bottom line related to money!) Count your self lucky, maybe even blessed, if you are not placed in a semi-private room with a cell mate who attempts to escape and in so doing "set off the bed alarm." Around two o'clock in the morning, when just drifted off to sleep, these things sound like a Jumbo Jet crash landing in the room. 'Bout as soon you show a sign of being able of remaining stable there is a transfer to a Rehab Hospital to make available a bed for a person leaving intensive care.

Rehab hospitals can be places which causes patients to wonder where all the little "Hitler's" (dictators) rehabbing you came from.

They have a large collection of them just looking for the opportunity to say "you can't do that" and stuff. The night life scene gets worse instead of improving too. Bright lights are turned on in your face at midnight by someone (idiot) who ask if you need ice water. Vampires sneak in around three o'clock (morning) to suck several tubes of blood from you. You soon start to thinking about ways of breaking out, even to the point of being "kicked out" for disobeying rules. I spoke with one lady who tried it. She got some cigarettes and allowed herself get caught smoking. It didn't work however, as she had her "smokes" taken away from her and was put into house arrest wearing one on those bracelet things to prevent sneaking out.

Renee, I thank you for coming and spending several days and nights at the crucial time. Now you know "dear ole dad" can still be "grumpy." Don't worry, it is wearing off and I have been assured of getting through this "valve job replacement" with no permanent personality warping. Teresa is keeping close "tabs" on everything which gives you the feeling of being an "All State" customer. JB you are absolutely correct about the curved keyboard once accustomed to it. I am back using the old one. Wanda left the wireless things at home. Actually, "dial-up" is all that is available where I am at now.

Written somewhere on the thin pages of the Christian Bible is where God said "it is not good for man to live alone", and he made a wo-man (Ish-AH) for a counterpart, often stated or understood as wife. Wanda comes every day if only for an hour or two. Often she will bring something special to eat, and will tidy-up the room some. She brought over the computer equipment and got it up and running. I look forward to the cheerful greeting each time she walks into the room. I want bore you with the other ten-thousand reason why I appreciate her. Sometimes I even ask myself why I should be so fortunate, more like blessed, to have a wife such as she.

Need to try the sleep thing before the vampires starts sweep in the room so I am out of here for now. kp

The Reminiscence Magazine

Here is your mail from Wandaland where the cows are always hungry and never give us any milk.

Well here it is the start of another hot lazy Saturday. Lot of chores which can wait until it is cooler, say what? Winter comes and it will be to cold! My reading has slacked off a smart since I need a "spy glass" to do a lot of it with. However "on account" of not being in the mood to do stuff I decided to read a little in my "Reminisce" Magazine which showed up in the mail box a few days ago.

I started to flip pages and right there on page 3 was a picture of a Belvedere Plymouth touring car sporting a "Swamp Cooler." Back in those day I finally became prospers enough to buy (a second hand) one from the junk yard. Were I ever in "tall cotton" and "the envy" of folks driving along with windows down and their little front air scoops windows capturing the wind. Yep, I and brother Ossed had a Mercury that had a sun visor too but we never had one of those prism things to alert us when the traffic signal turned to green. Fast forwarding a bit, times were after being a guest of Uncle Sam a few years and getting some book learning, itchy feet done took over and I scraped together coins to take hold of a 55 98holiday with all the bells and whistles and an A/C which made it seem like winter time. Wow, my monthly car payment then was about what it cost for a tank full of gasoline now days.

Just on over to page 6 there is an article on "Road side tourist attractions made long car trips fun." My how that was true, even the road signs as well. Perhaps there are those of you who remember the "Burma Shave" signs placed on fence posts. Old route 66, where the Camel humped to pleased had a lot of attractions. I done hear tell if'en ye drive parts left of old 66 it is a trip along memory lane for us older folks. Maybe someday I'll be doing that just for the heck of it, but sometime after going to Nashville to the "Grand Ole Opera." Still debating that one, on account it aint to much country anymore.

Another magazine for intellectuals such as I is the "Good Old Days." Its cover has a picture of the old hand pump gas dispenser with the glass jar marked off in gallons on top. Lot of stories and pictures in this one as well, but I want bore y'all with them. Talking "shore enough" these are interesting magazines.

Wanda is being the bread machine today. She is trying to out engineer me on it, I think. Last week I used 50% wheat flour and Splenda. She probably doesn't realize it, but when perfection is reached, there is only one way left, less good-er. Course the case isn't closed on that.

It was sometime last year when I stopped at a yard sale (garage sale to you townies) and bought a large stack of old, and I am talking old, old, records, the big 33 speed kind. There are more songs than beans in the pork-n-beans can and for sure pork.

The Reminiscence Magazine

Wanda just happens to be a person who keeps everything, and we have a "Victrola" of sorts. There is one of Mother Mae Bell Carter. What I am getting around to say, she bought me a birthday present (2 months early) which is a gismo which will copy all these records, tapes, etc, on to CDs. So, perhaps today or tomorrow I will sort out records to copy. Have to go to Wally World and get some blank disks and do a little practicing I suppose.

Tim, your superscription to the reminisces magazine was renewed. Renee, we are excited about your plans for next year. Other happenings here at Wandaland are about as solid as "fish net hosiery." Renee, we finally got around to eating the fruit cake you brought back from "somewhere" a trip or so ago and it sure was good. We are keeping the pretty can it came in on the shelf will all the other junk from here and there. Need to go to draft with this and do something before depositing in the "out box."

Here it is Sunday afternoon and Wanda's bread does run a close second, ha. She made a pan of rolls which never lasted until supper time. It all went very good today at lunch as she worked on a brisket, cooking it slow last night. That woman is a chef in the kitchen, a diplomat in the living room and bed room, a real sweetheart.

RFD-TV was real good last night, had Bobby Bare on. You can turn in on Dish 231 at 8 P. M. and catch some pretty good Midwest Country Shows. It is now time to close the lid on the tool box, sling out the paint from the brush, and get transported back to where the cows are always hungry and don't get milked. The liver lip cat Ziegler, and mealy mouth dog Patches are taking the heat pretty good. Until next time best to wear a wide brim hat, dust for chickers, and keep the gun powder dry. kp

THE LAST TRAIL RIDE

You have news from Wandaland where the cows are always hungry and never get milked. Life is like a long dusty trail across the land you have come to know so well. The trail had its sandy and rocky spots. There were hills where you looked across the plains and saw the vast open land full of opportunities. There has been a number of watering holes along the way to keep you going. You have rode most of the trail over and over again except for the last few miles which lies ahead. It came time to pull up under the shade of a large oak tree and take from the saddle bag the last remaining piece of jerky to sooth the nagging hunger of the stomach. The hat is flung against the chaps of the leg to shake off the dust just before giving the faithful horse loose reins to graze.

Seated on the ground with the back against the tree, thinking a bit on what might be expected at the end of the trail a squirrel seemed to appear from out of nowhere and commenced to nibble on an acorn. Then my eyes were drawn to a white rabbit which came running up, stopped and took a short look and went on its way to where ever it was going. Being in the "frame of mind" of what life is about, I thought a little of what it was like for these two creatures. I had always thought their main concerns were food for the day and not being dinner for a predator. I wanted to think life had more meaning than this for them, and then it came to me this is the way it is to be.

It was only a short time when my thought gravitated back to my trail ride. Lot of others commenced the ride with me. Some rode faster ahead and some turned away on trails to other places. I thought about facts of an old trail "hand." Unlike "old soldiers" old trail riders don't "fade away." True there is little "peer pressure" along the last miles of the way. Old trail riders are not like old truck drivers. Old truck drivers just keep on driving with a new "Peter:" built, tractor that is while still wearing cowboy dress boots.

Then my thoughts turned to "what has life been about." I can not say the world has been much better or worse since the day I rode away from the bunk house. Was it because of things in the past agonized and worried over which have seen me to be sitting in the shade of this old oak tree while recognizing the winter years hace arrived? Probably so, but still there was speculation while sitting and resting a spell in the shade what if there had there been less concern about food, not just for the day but for the year. And yes there have been predators which I allowed, but were they necessary?

There are a few "old saying" (possibly even proverbs) which I seem to like. It has been said people are born, grow up and marry the cousin next door; they become a Baptist and join a political party, grow old, die and live happier afterwards. Life has been said to be about "apple pie, Chevrolet, two hole moon houses in the back and lots of curtain climbers to boss around.

When I think of the billions and billions of people before me, many in this same country I sometimes ask of myself, "just who am I anyway?"

To my government I am known by a nine digit number. They will take notice of me should I fail to "fork over" money to them. When I check in at a hospital, to help spread wealth and purchase someone a Mercedes, the first question is "what is your social?" What they are actually asking is how do we know you?

But just who am I, and for what purpose? Why was I privileged (if that be the case) to be born in this country instead of another? These are indeed "hard" questions and it causes some people's brains go loco attempting to sort it all out.

Somewhere written on one of those thin pages of the Authorized King James Version of the Bible is stated people who so choose may have their names (not a number) written in the Lamb's (Jesus') book of life. Recon I was a little slow about "getting it" I did come to believe (act) the main thing about the trail ride is having the gap open when one reaches the end of the trail.

Pondering on stuff caused me to remember another saying, which preachers like to say now and again which is: "you can't take with you when you ride through the gate, but you can send it on ahead. A Brinks truck has never been known to follow a body to "boot hill." Yeah I know, on them thin pages in the front of the book it "talks" about laying up treasures, and I have pondered on what kind of treasures. I have had the notions my mansion would be furnished so once again what is a treasure that would be useful after riding on in? A treasure is something of much value and those thin pages also says "what can or would you give in exchange of your soul?" (There is nothing of equal value.) Souls are the most important things in life. Now if there are to be rewards at the end of the trail ride, would not souls a person help to the gate be rewarded?

Now my thoughts are back to what is life about? Once conclusion reached is it is about getting our names wrote in the "Book of Life." I have heard folks say since there will be no sorrows, disappointment or envy in the place they call heaven, there should be no concerns of rewards. As the "Pilgrim" says "its mind boggling." We are told people who choose to ride on in will get a "complete makeover" on account of uncleanness before being allowed to ride in. It just seems like the more I think I understand, the much less I truly do. It seems to me like, as an example, as we sometime hear "different strokes for different folks." It only takes a "Mac Junior" to satisfy a three year old and it is devoured before the adult finishes off a triple burger. (no envy or jealousy). Another thing I pondered on under the oak tree is that life is about increasing a person's capacity to enjoy the place called heaven according to how we treat others we come in contact with.

Yes, there are those who choose to ride a beautiful thorough-bred stallion having the finest saddle blanket and saddle. The saddle bags are full of jerky and several canteens of water hang on to the saddle. They wear the finest chaps and Stetson hat. They sit tall in the saddle and when they ride on in they wish they had given out of their abundance to the needy people along the trail. They chose to not send it on ahead, and they couldn't bring it on in with them.

If I understand the writing on those thin pages of "The Book" a person is committing the same wrong that has one thin dime to spare and kept is for him self as someone who has thousands and does like wise.

You have un-doubly heard of people who keep digging the hole they are in until it is too deep to get out of. And buckaroo that is what ye might call despair or being in a predicament. And so it is with much of the trail ride. The lyrics of a song probably sums up the trail ride accurately with words which speak of a time we won't care to know about stuff of this life anymore. Do we really need to understand or just hold His hand along the trail?

And folks I recon that is all I have to say about that before riding on from Wandaland where the cows are always hungry and never milked. Y'all be sure to inspect the blanket before saddling up and riding the fences. kp

Scenes in Alaska

Alaska Cabin in the Wilderness

Road to Mr. McKinley, AK

The Columbia Glacier

The Winter Refrigerator

Scenes in Ireland

Guiness at Fitzpatricks

Ireland Country Road

Quite man Bridge Ireland

Vacation Castle in Ireland

Scenes in New Zealand

A Park in New Zealand

Alan & Diane's Farm

Mountain on North Island, NZ

Road on South Island, NZ

Scenes in Yukon & B.C. Canada

Diamond Tooth Gerties Saloon

Moose near Anch., AK

Old AlCan Road Bridge

Show at Gerties's Saloon

REFLECTIONS

OF

1930—1940

FOLKLORE SHORT STORIES

THE OLD PLACE

HOMECOMEING

CHURCH AT LILBERT

THE DINING TABLE

GRANDMA IS COMING

THE RADIO

CHRISTMAS ON THE FARM

HALLOWEEN

EASTER EGG HUNTS

SPECIAL DAYS

SUMMER NIGHTS

STUDYING SCHOOL LESSONS

THE FIRST BICYCLE

THE MATTRESS FACTORY

THE GOATS

THE POTS & PAN MAN

THE JUNK MAN

THE MARTIN BOX

FARMING

FOOD OF THE 1930'S

CANNING DAYS

WASH DAY

THE WAR

CUSHING

OUR NEIGHBORS

Kinchen Parker

1942 Parker Place

THE OLD PLACE

In the summer of 1980 my family and I flew from Anchorage, Alaska to Dallas, Texas on vacation. We were to visit relatives in several East Texas and Southeast Texas towns. Estleen Ayres, a sister of mine, lived on a farm in East Texas. Our kids were looking forward to going there for a few days because there was a horse to ride. There was also something about going to town when you live in the country. It is just not the same as going "downtown" when you live in town. They also talked of helping haul hay for cows and doing various other chores associated with farm life.

The day we arrived in Dallas was beautiful. There were a few scattered clouds high in the sky, and it was a bit warm for early morning. Another sister, Dorothy Hurta, and her husband Edwin, lived in Dallas, they met us at the airport. We spent the day and night with them, and the next day borrowed one of their cars to continue the vacation. As we drove out of Dallas towards deep East Texas the services stations and fast food places changed to trees and green pastures where cattle grazed. A music tape, which had been left in the car, was discovered when we first arrived in the countryside. It was a collection of songs by the Sattler brothers. It is difficult to say which was enjoyed the most, the tape or the pleasant drive. I suppose each enhanced the other. All of the songs were folklore and there was two, which became favorites immediately. A few days later when we visited the site of the Old Parker Place these song came to mind. One song related a number of events in a person life when he was a young boy. The story was told how "you can't go home to the good times." Another song told a story about a man who went to visit a school he attended as a young boy many years before. He remembered the school "bully" and still wished he could give him a punch in the nose. The water fountains seemed much taller then. He thought of his fifth grade teacher and realized she really wasn't terrible at all. He looked at the building from the playground and thought it would be very easy to put a ball right through the office window now. "Time changes everything" is just another way of saying things change with time. As indicated in song, things may seem to change, but we are the ones who change.

As I walked over the ground at the Old Place I though about how far the water well seemed to be from the house. There was the chicken house, the barn, the old car shed, the outdoor outhouse, and the blacksmith shop. I tried to picture in my mind where each had been located, and realized they were not as far away from the house as I had remember them to be. The small grove of pine trees down the hill behind the house had to have been much closer than my childhood memory of the distance away.

Words would be most inadequate to state the hundreds of memories, perhaps even thousand, associated with this old place by other family members and me. At least fourteen children lived at the Old Parker Place at one time or another. As I listen to conversations, it became apparent there were a wide variety of memories, and any attempt to record just the significant ones would be a tremendous undertaking.

When thinking of the Old Parker Place and life of the 1930's, I am grateful life allows a person to remember more of the good things than the unpleasant ones. By some standards we were poor, as the great depression had made its mark on most country people. However, by standards of more importance we were rich. Our clothes were patched, but they were clean. Homemade quilts covered the beds. Food was simple, but enough with some to spare to someone hungry.

The Old Parker Place was much more than a house with a few scattered building, it was home. It was a place where mistakes were allowed and often made. Everyone felt secure there even with no locks on doors and windows opened. It was a place of training; a place where adult neighbors were referred to as Mr. or Mrs. Children was taught to rise and offer their chair to adults who entered the room. The house had a fireplace, wood heaters, and a wood cook stove. A child home from school could always find a snack in the "safe" to eat before changing into work clothes. A mailbox, usually without a lid, stood in front by the road. And a rope-tire swing hung from a limb of the huge oak tree beside the house. "Grace" was asked before every meal and we believed in God to supply the necessities of life. Flowers grew beside the garden fence and there was a pet dog which we loved It was a place where we experienced the joy of many discoveries, and learned things which were unpleasant. I suppose that the Old Parker Place, with a tin and wood shingle roof, unpainted walls, and water bucket with face pan on a shelf at the front porch, occupies a special place in the memory of each person who once lived there.

HOMECOMEING

There was never an exclusive time set by the Parkers for a reunion where relatives of the family would attend. The immediate family and several relatives did get together for Christmas. There was a summer day each year when the community of Lilbert and the church set aside as "home coming" day. The Parker side of the family observed this day as all of daddy's siblings had lived there. Each year all of the daddy's brothers and sisters came, even several that were living in Dallas. Some of our aunts and uncles would spend a night or two with us. The home coming attracted many famous gospel singers and the day was spent singing, listening to the quartets, visiting with relatives and friends. Sometimes there would be a singing school held at the church a week or so before the homecoming. It was a time when women tried to "outdo" themselves with cooking. A wire mesh table of about three feet wide and fifty feet long would not hold all the food that was brought. A number of people who were seeking public office came and handed out their "candidate cards." Children collected the cards and traded with each other much as kids that collect baseball cards do today. Then, as in now, the idea was to get as many different cards as possible. A refreshment stand was operated throughout the day. The local Coca-Cola and Dairyland Ice Cream companies donated employee's labor and profits went towards the upkeep of the Redland Cemetery. Cokes and Dixie Ice cream Cups were a nickel. The inside lid of the Dixie Cup ice cream had a picture of a movie star on it. These too were collected by kids. Before the day ended it was announced several tims when the community would come together to work as a group in the Redland Cemetery.

The Robert Neel family (relatives of Mother's side) was also early settlers of the community and a few came to the homecoming. However, every few years they would hold a family reunion at the "Friendship Church.' The church was located on the road to Nat, a mile or so from the Cushing/Lilbert "Y". Many years later it was moved to the Looneyville community and remodeled. It was the custom to have some "harp" singing at this reunion. This is singing where notes are sung instead of the words while keeping time of the hymn. There was no musical instrument played, and not more than three or four songs were sung this way. Kinchen was known to participate in this singing some and seemed to enjoy it a lot.

The reunions of the 1930's were considerabley different from the ones in 1980. They were not limited to relatives, and were generally considered a public community function open to anyone who wanted to attend. They were a time to renew old acquaintances, to fellowship with friends and neighbors and to learn about various events in the lives of people you didn't have close or everyday contact with.

I suppose homecomings and reunions were as exciting to everyone as a young person's first trip to the circus. The happiness of the day had a way of diminishing as family members departed for their homes, and wondering if there would be another and who would be missing the next time.

Lilbert Church

CHURCH AT LILBERT

Going to and attending the small country church at Lilbert was always an experience for me, though I can't say it was something I always enjoyed. I was five or six years old at the time I remember. The church was about three miles from our home. Sometimes we walked and other times the mule team would be hitched to the wagon and we rode. One thing I didn't enjoy was returning home at night when I was very sleepy, especially when we walked. When we rode in the wagon I wished Mama would just let me sleep in the wagon the rest of the night after getting home. Mama always wanted to get to church early although that didn't happen each time. The main reason was to get a good seat and have a place under the beach for us kids to sleep. It was a time for families to visit as well, as many families came early for those purposes, Quilts were taken and placed under the benches to sleep on as it was not uncommon for services to last three to four hours. It would be close to midnight when we got back home. Actually there wasn't a lot of sleeping that took place as the services included a lot of singing old hymns as "When the Roll is Called Up Yonder" and a testimonial time. During the testimonial time there would be "shouting" (loud praising to the Lord) and "dancing" (a holy dance without a partner) would "break-out" several times. It was dangerous for kids to be sleeping in the open, as they could be accidentally trampled. I do not recall this ever happened to me.

Revivals were referred to as "protracted meetings." The original contract was for two weeks but they often lasted three to four weeks. Two preaches came, one a Methodist and the other a Baptist, who took turns preaching every other night.

Many times the preachers would come to our house for dinner (lunch), and sometimes spent the night as well. Their visits usually insured a chicken dinner, mashed potatoes and a berry cobbler. Converts during the revival were baptized in a pond on the last Sunday afternoon. The Methodist had no objection to be immersed same as the Baptists. There were lots of people on the banks and a few in the water as well to witness the baptisms. These were climatic events that marked the end of the revivals.

Inside up front of the church, on the right had side were several benches referred to as the "Amen corner." Older men, perhaps deacons and elders, sat here (with out their wives) "amening" the preachers as they preached, letting them know the sermon message was being agreed with. On the opposite side in the left corner was where the women (mostly wives) sat. In the center and back a way was benches for "lead singers" as there was no such thing as a choir. Between these benches and the platform of the podium was a long narrow bench having no back, which was the altar, a place for prayer, weeping, confession and being "born again." There was never a paid pianist or song leader. Offerings were taken at each night revival meeting and was divided between the preachers. Sometimes when little offering had been given, a special offering would be taken at the end of the revival.

A ministry for teenagers referred to as B.Y.P.U. (Baptist Young People Union) was started. (This was later to be "Training Union" and "Church training" which encompassed other age groups. Buford, an older brother, claimed to have attended a lot. However mama sometime found out he didn't always make it there, probably going to a house party dance instead, as he would come home very late at night.

THE DINING TABLE

Our dining table was a long table built by my father. In the beginning it could easily seat twelve to fourteen people. The table was cut off a foot or two each time a couple of the children got married and moved out. It was shortened a few times before my family decided it was the proper length.

When daddy was home he always sat at the head of the table, and the oldest boy would take his place should he be gone away.

Mama sat next to daddy at the table and the children sat on benches next to her, beginning with the youngest. The older members of the family sat in cane and raw hide bottom chairs on the opposite side, usually in order as well. With ten older siblings I was about twelve years old before my turn came to sit in a chair at the dining table.

We always had a bright table cloth. It was more of linoleum tham a cloth and it had pictures of fruit or flowers on it. Because it was heavily used it had to be replaced every two or three years.

Discipline was rigid at the table. A clean face and hands were required and we had to be completely dressed, except for shoes. Daddy always asked for the blessing of the food before every meal. Adults were served before children. Small children were required to say "may I have" and after receiving it say "thank you" for the food they wanted to eat. Children were not to ask for the last piece or helping of the food. When we were behaved improperly we had to leave the table, and sometimes that meant going without the particular meal. Usually Mama would fix us a plate and give it to us later provided we had not acted to badly.

Zude Virginia Hillard

GRANDMA IS COMING

Grandma Parker lived with her daughter (our aunt Lena) in Dallas, Texas for many of her last years. During that time she would come and spend a week or more with us almost every summer. Once in a while she sent a postal card explaining she wouldn't be able to come for the annual visit. Everyone would be "so" disappointed because we dearly loved her and looked forward to the visits. More often we received a card announcing the day she would arrive and we could hardly wait for her arrival.

Aunt Lena usually brought grandma, and sometime aunt Gertha came as well. It would not be unusual for them to bring Aunt Callie too. Our aunts always looked us kids over and would "go on" how we had grown the past year. We were required to hug and kiss grandma but I hated kissing my aunts. I was more than glad when it was decided that I was too old for that. I suppose my resistance had something to do with the decision.

Extensive housecleaning always took place before grandma came. This was about the only time I helped. Usually the girls did the inside work and the boys had the outside chores.

Mama said many times how much she thoroughly enjoyed Grandma Parker visits, and she never required any kind of special treatment. As mama said, "she was no trouble at all." Grandma liked to help with the cooking and do things like shelling peas.

She would shell them in her apron. Most of all I think she enjoyed sitting in the rocking chair by the radio and listing to the Long Ranger with Ossed and me.

At the end of every visit Grandma Parker gave Ossed and me a fifty-cent piece. At one of the visits, Estleen, a sister slightly older than I, made a remark to mama about being left out. Grandma didn't intend to do that or be that way. I think she just saw Ossed and me as special grandkids. Mama said "something" to Grandma and from that year on she had a fifty-cent piece for Estleen as well. The giving of fifty-cent pieces came to a halt when we became older.

One day we received dreadful news that Grandma Parker has passed away. I suppose she had been sick for a little while as it seemed that mama and daddy was expecting the bad news. I remember going down to the barn that day, crawling up in the hayloft and crying a lot. While I didn't recognize it then a special family tradition hnd come to an end.

THE RADIO

The battery-powered radio did much to keep rural America informed about the rest of the country. We took a weekly newspaper, which came by mail. It had news from communities of the county as well as other local and national news, but it was generally old. The radio, on the other hand, provided up-to-date news, music, and other live entertainment.

The first radio I remember in my family was purchased in 1937 when I was six years old and in the first grade. I am sure radios, especially crystal sets, had been owned previously as pianos and telephones were owned before the great depression.

Our radio was a table model, though floor consoles were popular by those who could afford one. A long wire antenna and ground rod were needed for best reception. The battery contained many one-cells and was expensive.

We always knew when the radio battery would soon need replacing, as the volume would get weak and then weaker. My family thought placing the radio at a low volume would prolong the life of the battery, but of course that wasn't true. The radio was not allowed to be on unless someone was consciously listening to it. Needless to say, kids were supervised as to what could be listen to.

The girls in the family enjoyed listening to "Ma Perkings" and "Portia Blake Faces Life." As one might expect, soap companies sponsored many programs as well as cereal companies. Oxydol and Rinso were the two most popular brands advertised for soap, and Wheaties for cereal. The boys listened to "Jack Armstrong" (the All-American boy), the "Lone Ranger" and mysteries such as "The Shadow." Everyone enjoyed listening to "Amos and Andy" and the "Grand OLE Opera." Mama especially enjoyed listing to Sam Morris, the "Voice of Temperance." It was a program against drinking whiskey and always commenced with sounds of cars crashing. Old Sam finally persuaded enough people to send him money whereby he was able to have his own radio station. Much of the nighttime listening was tuned to station "XEG" "The Voice of North America", a clear channel station. There was a lot of "static" (inferences) in those day with the AM (amplitude modulated frequency) radio stations. Station KSKY, in Dallas had a number of fifteen-minute preacher programs that became favorites of mama. The only music we were allowed to listen to was "string instrument music." Music that was played with wind instruments was not allowed to be listened to. It was referred to as "horn music", and I believe mama considered it to be sinful. She changed her mind about this in later years but never really cared for it. I remember listening to Hawaiian music and enjoying it a lot. My dream was to go to Hawaii one day as I thought it would be exciting and adventurous. The dream came true much later as I was the guest of "Uncle Sam" in the navy. Watching the Hawaiian girls dance and sing, engaging in other Hawaiian culture was exciting, but it was not like I had imagined as a young boy at home.

CHRISTMAS ON THE FARM

Several months before Christmas the children commenced to look for way to earn money to buy presents. Money was also needed to purchase fireworks for Christmas Eve celebration. Many hours were spent, mostly in variety stores, looking for presents that would be "just right" for members of our family. The presents were wrapped with paper from previous years, "fancy wrapping paper", newspaper or paper from a brown bag.

A tree was selected the first day school was out for the holidays. The axe was sharpened and two or three kids went through the woods to find a tree that would be just the right shape and size. After many hours of looking and comparing, a tree was finally selected. Sometimes a pine was selected and sometimes a cedar. I never knew why but the tree was often placed in the boy's bedroom, which was referred to as the "little room." The tree stand was always built from wood boards. As there was no electricity, there were no tree lights. Stringing popcorn and making chains from paper colored by crayons made up most of the tree decorations. A second trip was made to the woods to look for holly and holly berries, which were used to make wreaths with the berries strung for tree decoration.

Christmas was a time when all the married children, with their children, came home. Many relatives also came on Christmas Eve and Christmas Day. Mattresses were placed on the floor for a bed. Kids and a few adults, slept on the floor, sometime three and four to a bed, depending on their size.

The old quilt box, a huge wooden box with a lid, was where quilts and blankets were kept. It was also a good hiding place for Christmas stocking toys which had been purchased well in advance of Christmas. Some toys were bought on Christmas Eve morning when mama and daddy would go to Cushing to buy candy and nuts. Daddy always bought a box (bushel) of apples and lots of oranges. Candy, oranges and nuts

166

were for the stockings but the box of apples was placed under the bed, where often kids would "sneak" one to eat.

The entire fireplace mantle had stocking "hung by the chimney with care". Most stockings were mama's long brown stockings, some with a hole in the tow. An apple or orange was placed in the ones with the holes to prevent other small thing falling out.

A not so very short list was placed over several of the Christmas stocking for Santa to see and hopefully leave what was asked. Sometime the toys were left up to Santa too. Naturally Santa did not always score perfectly each time but his record was good, and all the kids were well pleased. By the time dinner was ready on Christmas Day most of the kids were rather full on apples as we seldom had apples at any other time. One year Santa left a big shiney truck under my nephew Charles's stocking. I got up real early, probably around four in the morning and went to see what Santa had brought. I saw the truck and wanted it so bad that I took it and placed it under my stocking and went back to bed. The next morning it was back under Charles' stocking and I couldn't understand how it got back there. There was also a time when brother James decided there wasn't a Santa and he refused to hang a stocking. All of our faith was restored the next morning when one of his pants legs was tied up and filled with toys, fruit and candy. I think James believed for a little while longer.

Probably no less than thirty people ate Christmas dinner at the Old Parker Place. Weeks before Christmas three or four chickens were put in a coop and fed. We had chicken and dressing, ham, fruit salads, and no less than ten pies and cakes of different kinds. Several coconuts were bought and grated for some of the pies and cakes. A coconut might find its way in one of the stockings if there was an extra one. Coconut pie was a favorite of many of the people and so was a cake made with black walnuts.

There were simply to many people to sit at the dining table to eat. Everyone gathered around and the blessing of the food was asked, usually by our oldest sister Ovie, Children were helped with their plates, and sent out to the porch or to other rooms to eat. The unloading of the tree, which is giving of presents, was done shortly after dinner (lunch) on Christmas Day. Everyone who could, gatherd around the tree and Ovie, the oldest, always said a prayer. As a child I always though her prayers were a lot to long, but I suppose that I was a bit anxious. It was also the custom for Ovie to remove the presents from the tree, announce whom they were for and whom it was from. It took a long time to distribute all of the presents. The pretty wrapping paper, which there was little of, was saved with the ribbons and placed in a box for use the next Christmas.

The Christmas tree, which was once pretty, became bare and unattractive without the presents and decorations. When it was taken down the next day after Christmas Day we would realized the holiday season had ended sooner than we would have liked for it to.

HALLOWEEN

Halloween was a special time for us. We enjoyed playing games in the yard by the light of a bonfire, and roasting wieners and marshmallows. As with many events, neighbor kids joined in the festivities. One year daddy took a white bed sheet and slipped down the road undetected. He then came towards us, while making a scary sound, covered in the sheet. I remember being afraid, though I didn't want to be, and finally ran like the other kids.

The school at Cushing had a Halloween Carnival each year. There was cakewalks, apple dunking, fishing and other traditional games. The climax was the crowning of a Halloween Queen. Each vote cost one cent and the girl who got the most votes was crowned. I didn't always get to attend the carnival, as I didn't have money. It cost ten cents to ride the bus to Cushing, and there was a small charge for the activities. When I was very young someone was needed to "look after" me, and there were few volunteers.

EASTER EGG HUNTS

We were educated concerning the religious aspects of Easter, but we still looked forward to the egg hunts on Easter Sunday. Two or three dozen hen eggs would be boiled and colored with crayons. and a nest was made in the pasture where the eggs were first placed in it. One of the older kids would take the younger ones through the pasture looking under every bush for the nest until it was found. One year we got very tired hunting it and was about to give up when it was found. Many years later I learned the eggs weren't quite ready and there was stalling for time to get them all colored. The nest of eggs were collected and carried to the house for later hunts. There was never a time when any of the kids had an Easter basket, and I can't ever remember that was important either. The excitement of Easter was thrilling and a basket could not have made it better.

After Sunday dinner (lunch) kids from the neighborhood would come, and there would be Easter egg hunts in the front yard. Everyone had to go inside, and someone was assigned to see there was no peeping while the adults hid the eggs.

Finding Easter eggs hid in the yard was a lot more fun than finding the original big nest in the pasture that morning. There might be two or three hunts in the front yard before the adults became tired. A little begging could usually bring about one more. The eggs would then be divided up among all the kids.

The community church at Lilbert sponsored a community Easter egg hunt the years I was growing up. I remember going to it once and not enjoying it very much. There were too many kids and the hunt was in a large field. I think the adults in the community got a "kick" out of it, as a number of then participated in one way or another.

SPECIAL DAYS

My younger brother Ossed and I experienced the special joy of giving when we gave our parents small gifts on Mother's and Father's days.

Daddy didn't use a billfold until his later years. Instead, he carried a small pocket purse in his front pocket. It held coins and folded bills. On Father's day we usually gave him a pocket purse or a dollar pocket watch. Neither one seem to last from one Father's day to the next.

A fresh bouquet of flowers, usually "Four O'Clocks, were picked on Mother's Day, put in a pint fruit jar, and placed on the dinning table by Ossed and me on Mother's Day. We always set the morning breakfast table for Mama with all the plates turned upside down. Under her plate we put a nice handkerchief purchased at the Lilbert store. She never failed to act surprised even thought it was a bit habitual for us to do that. In those days women carried handkerchiefs in their hands virtually every place that went in public, especially to church. Some years we also did the morning dishes and made sure the kitchen stove wood box was full of wood.

SPECIAL NIGHTS

It seemed as if there were special times for everything in the summer. There was a time to canning food, a time to work in the garden, a time to harvest the crops and a time to cut and lay-in fireplace wood for winter heating of the house.

As farm children we were required to work quite diligently, but we were never to tired to play at night after a "long hard day of work." Most nights Mama had to call us kids in at bed time, and no one wanted to be the last person to wash their feet in the "foot-tub" before going to bed. To be caught going to bed with dirty feet would bring about some form of discipline. One could fairly well be assured of being caught by Mama too as one of the others would be a 'tattletale" and somehow Mama always knew when she was being lied to.

Many nights were very special. Our teenage twin sisters played guitars and sang, and the rest of us would often sing with them as well. Homemade, hand-cranked, ice cream was made on some of those special nights. Milk was kept cool in the water well for a couple of days to have enough. The wooden ice cream buckets were soaked for a couple days also, so the planks would swell and close the cracks of the wooden bucket, otherwise the salty icy sludge water would leak out. The mixture in the inner container that was being turned wouldn't freeze. A hundred pounds of ice would be purchased from the icehouse in Cushing during the day and kept from melting by placing a lot of "toe-sacks" (burlap bags) around it before nightfall. Often times neighbors would be invited to the ice cream making, It was not unusual for fifteen and twenty gallons of ice cream to be made with the hand-crank freezers. Usually the kids would take turns with the turning of the hand-cranks.

There was a show house (Movie Theater) at Cushing in those days but none of the country folks in our "neck of the woods" ever went. We were not allowed to go day or night. My parents taught us that it was a sin to go to a movie. I just accepted that until I got much older and "slipped-off' to see one. It took a long time for me to get away from that teaching, but today I would have to agree that most movies are sinful entertainment.

In addition to singings on the porch at nights, having ice cream parties, there was an occasional weenie roast at night when we could afford to buy weenies. We played games by bon fires frequently. One of the games that everyone seemed to enjoy was "stealing sticks." We would divide up the number of kids into two groups. A line would be drawn across the yard and a pile of sticks placed on each side of the line equal distances away. The objective was to cross over the line and make it to the pile of sticks without being tagged. If you were tagged you were out of the game.

The main objective was for one side to be able to collect all sticks on their side. Everyone had to stand at the line until someone crossed over and then they could be chased and tagged. It would not be unusual for team members of each side to be crossing over at the same time, stealing sticks before one side was declared the winner.

There would be some nights when the yard would have a lot of flying bugs that gave off an occasionally glow. While I guess we never knew the correct name of them we simply called them "Lightening Bugs" because they seem to produce a small light on and off as the flew about. We thought perhaps that was their way of signaling to each other their location. While it may or may not have been, it sure allowed us to catch them and put them in a fruit jar.

Kids of the 1980's who have movies, televisions, video games and malls to "hang" with friends in, can sometime be heard to say they are "bored" and have nothing to do. Perhaps the "generation gap" is just too wide for me to connect.

STUDYING SCHOOL LESSONS

Our family had a name for every room in our house at the Old Parker Place. The names didn't always indicate the function of the room as they do today, and the ones that did were stated different. The "stove room" was the kitchen, the "eating room" was the dining room. I suppose that country people never though of eating as dining. The "fireplace room", where a fireplace was located, was the living room. Other rooms in the house at Lilbert were the hall, the little room and the big room were bedrooms. The big room could easily hold three double size beds, and once did. The headboards and footboards were generally made of iron, and are considered to be antiques today.

We studied our school lesson in the big room at night, after supper and all the chores were done. Daddy built us a large table and some benches to use. Several kids could be seen sitting at the table studying by the light of a kerosene lamp. There was a wood heater in the wintertime to keep us warm, and sometime it became too warm. It was not unusual for the stovepipe (flue-pipe) to become cherry red from all the heat the heater was producing.

I did not like studying in the big room with the rest of my brothers and sisters, because they wanted me to keep quiet. I would ask a lot of question and ask for help a lot too. They were busy with studying their own lessons. In the winter I would often go to the fireplace and sit beside the churn of milk mama had placed there, and study by the light of the fire in the fireplace. If mama was in the room, perhaps churning as she often did at night, she would help me with my spelling, arithmetic and reading.

THE FIRST BICYCLE

Older brother James purchased the first bicycle in the family of the younger generation of Lilbert Parkers. He purchased it for 50 cents from a girl in Cushing whose last name was Baker. As I recall it required a little "fixing-up" but that was no "never mind" for James. It didn't take him very long to be the best bicycle mechanic around. He could re-spoke wheels perfectly, and make old gears in the rear drive wheel run smooth and easy to peddle as though the bike was brand new. Learning to ride the bicycle was one of the greatest thrills I had as a young person. After it had been mastered, I couldn't ride it enough. Every once in while I can re-capture some of the feeling as my mind drifts back to those years.

The bicycle had small tires, which we referred to as "clincher tires." It wasn't the best bike for dirt roads, but dirt roads were all there was in the community. One time when Dorothy, an older sister, was riding it on the road in front of the house, which was extremely rough with deep ruts that cars and wagons had made. Dorothy lost control, fell and bumped her head. It took a few days for her to recover as she suffered a minor case of amnesia. She acted very strange during her convalescence.

We were supposed to get permission from James to ride the bike. That I did not always do. However, he got me to perform a number of his chores by allowing me to ride it for a while. It wasn't long afterwards, though it seemed like forever, another bike came in the family. Daddy gave Ossed $12 to purchase a bike from Lee Roy Self. This bike was a boy's bike whereas James' was a girl's bike. Ossed's bike had large tires but it was harder to mount and dismount.

THE MATTRESS FACTORY

Bed mattresses normally had cotton inside, although some had feathers, and the poorest of poor people sometime had corn shuck mattresses. Every few years the cotton mattresses would pack and become uncomfortable. The cotton was then taken out and fluffed. Sometimes it was accomplished by hand which required a lot of time and energy, Sometime a truck would come through the community collecting people's mattresses taking them to a factory for reworking. The old ticking would be replaced with new if the person desired, or they could retain the old. There were a lot of people who were reluctant to use this service, even though the cost was reasonable, for fear they would not get the original cotton or ticking back.

One year daddy decided to go into the mattress rework business. He had built a house for a man near Cushing and taken a lot of old machinery as his pay, and some of it was used to build his factory. It was made in the car shed, and the power source was an old Model-T truck in the back, which had a drive belt from a rear wheel to the machine.

There was considerable trouble in the beginning with the belt breaking and running off the pulley. After a number of days of building and testing the day finally came to see how it would work with cotton from a mattress. The "contraption" actually worked well, but only two mattresses were ever reworked, and they were our own. I don't think mama liked the idea much of having to sew ticking, and daddy hadn't given a lot of thought to picking up and delivering either. The mattress factory was eventually dismantled. I remember us kids playing on the old truck, which remained in the rear of the car shed for a number of years.

THE GOATS

For a few years daddy kept several goats in the pasture beside the house. They were kept primarily to help keep down the persimmon bushes which seem to grow abundantly in the pasture. There was one goat we named Billy because he butted people every chance he got. He knocked Ossed and me down a lot and would keep it up until an adult came and chased him away or we were able to escape. Ossed and I tried to ride some of the goats, and Ossed did make a pet out of one. He made it a harness of sorts, and the goat would pull him in a wagon.

A black man named Charlie Thomas, and his family lived not so far away from us on the same road. As small children we didn't know his surname, and we referred to him as "Negro Charlie. Mr. Thomas was rather old, so it seemed to us kids at the time, and he had a long beard we like to touch and feel.

Mr. Thomas had a large family and they always celebrated "Juneteenth" on June 19th of each year, the date blacks became free in the south. About a week before the

19th, and on a Sunday, Mr. Thomas would come to see daddy about buying a goat to barbecue for the occasion. It was always on a Sunday afternoon, as he knew there would be bargaining which would take most of the evening. Fifty cents would be daddy's first asking price. After an hour or so of bartering, the price would drop to twenty-five cents. The bartering would stop again for a while and other things talked about. Mr. Thomas would open up the bargaining again by saying "my chillen has to have a goat." The agreed price was usually around ten to fifteen cents for a goat, and it was always bought on "credit." I know the money was never paid, and if it had been offered daddy would have refused it. This event took place as long as we had goats. The Thomas family moved from the community and we lost contact with them and their "where abouts."

THE POT & PAN MAN

Each year a handyman who repaired pots and pans came by our house at Lilbert. The truck he traveled in was somewhat amusing. It had pots and pans and chicken coops with chicken in them hanging from his truck. The man took chickens, eggs or anything else of value for pay. The pots and pans he tried to fix were made of aluminum. Because they were very inexpensive, cheaply constructed from aluminum they developed holes in them with little use. The Pot Man would attempt to patch the holes but they nearly always leaked again just a few day's after he left.

If there weren't any pots or pans to repair he would sharpen scissors. One time mama allowed him to sharpen hers as she sewed a lot and they were dull. The man made them duller and mama had to wait a few days until daddy came home from a job to sharpen them before she could continue with her sewing. I do not believe it was the scissors, which held her up, as much as it was the old Singer foot pedal machine. The tension on the machine needed some adjusting, and mama let the man "tinker" with it too.

Peddlers (door to door salesmen) often came by selling all kinds of merchandise. Some sold Bibles and others pictures that would glow in the dark. They sold bedspreads or just about anything to make a dollar. There was one, which seemed to come by fairly often, selling flavorings, extracts and liniments which was guaranteed to cure just about anything a person had or would ever expect to have. There was one that peddled "over the counter" things such as "Three-sixes", 'Cardui' "Black draught" and elixirs remedies for hooping-cough and salves for seven-year itch. I don't remember if any of us had to be treated for lice or not.

Occasionally a hobo would come to the door asking to work in exchange for something to eat. I remember that my older brother Buford, who could be quite a prankster, did this once just for the "heck" of it, and stated that he got a real good meal for splitting a few sticks of wood. Turning hungry people away was something that country people didn't do even if a cold biscuit was all there was to offer. It was not a bit unusual for a covered wagon load of gypsies to camp on the side of the road near the house and beg. We thought we had to keep a "close eye" on them until they moved along.

THE JUNK MAN

Once a year a man would come through the community in his truck buying scrap iron, copper and aluminum. All year long several of the younger kids would "pile-up" old scrap. Walking all over the place looking for something to sell usually added a piece or two to the pile. We seldom found any copper or aluminum, and sometime scrap iron became scare as "hen's teeth", but generally there would be a modest pile of iron.

We had no idea when the junk man would come, only that he would, because he always did. He usually "showed-up" one day in the fall, about the time we had forgotten about it. The scrap was weighed with an old set of "Pea-Scales" hanging from the truck, and we were paid a penny or two per pound for it. The junk man coming by didn't last too many years. I don't know if it was because people ran out of old scrap iron to sell or if it just became unprofitable for him. The money we got, usually less than a dollar was divided among the kids who had contributed to the effort.

THE MARTIN BOX

A birdhouse was mounted on a slender tall pine pole in front of the house. The pole had to be replaced every two or three year. We referred to the birdhouse as "The Martin Box" as it was for their home to live in for a short time each year. Sparrows attempted to take over the birdhouse each year but we chased them away. When the sparrows came we ran them off with slingshots and pellet-guns. Every few years the house had to be replaced as it was never painted. There were not a lot of compartments (individual nesting rooms), perhaps four at the most. I got a special kind of satisfaction in helping make the birdhouses. I would imagine it was like the feeling a young boy would have helping his dad build his dog a house.

A highlight was when each spring the martins began to arrive. First, one or two would show up, and later more would corne. In the "dusk" of the evening our family would sit on the front porch and watch them fly about their house and perch on the porch. We could see them feeding their young ones, and sometimes a baby bird would fall out the house. It was fun to watch the small birds learn to fly. We always knew the fall season was about to change as the Martins would leave to some other place. While we knew we would miss them we also knew they would be back next year, as they always did.

FARMING

A small farmer's work of the 1930's was quite different than a farmer's work in the 1980's. Each day on our farm began when it was light enough to see in the fields. Mama would start cooking breakfast about 5:00 a.m. We stopped working in the fields when it began to get dark, and often finished the workday in the dark taking care of the animals and performing other chores. Daddy made a trip to the bank early spring, and everything that was owned, including cows, mules, farm implements, etc. were mortgaged to obtain money to buy seeds, fertilizer, and mule feed with. Had it not been illegal some families would have mortgaged a kid or two. A copy of the Farmer's Almanac hung on the wall by a nail near the fireplace. It contained a lot of information about farming and other useful things. It was looked at quite a bit during winter and early spring, but it was seldom followed.

Very few small farms had a tractor, so horses and mules were used to pull the farm implements in planting and cultivating. Daddy didn't like to own horses for farming, and I can remember having only one horse for a short time. Several things determined the kind of farm implement used in farming. First the kind of preparation of the field, the kind of crop, and if it was believed to have a wet or dry year. Farm tools such as disks, harrows, middle busters, turning plows, Georgia stocks, cultivators, planters, and fertilizers were used, all "mule powered."

When I was too young to work in the fields I had the job of carrying fresh drinking water to the workers in the fields. This was done once in the morning and once in mid-afternoon. If it was an extra hot day, and many were, two trips would be made in the afternoon, one a bit earlier and another a bit later than mid-afternoon. The water was carried in one-gallon syrup buckets, which had no lids. There were four rules to be followed. First, the water had to be fresh drawn from the well. I was never to be late arriving, trash was not allowed in the water and daddy was to receive a drink first. I would take a bucket of water in each hand and sometime the water would "slosh-out" while running to not be late. I would be sent back home for more water when there was not enough for everyone.

As I got older and commenced working in the fields, the days were long and hot. I was a lot more concerned about the heat than removing grass from around the plants. Occasionally during the day I looked up in the sky to see if there were any clouds near that might pass overhead to provide a shade for a while. When there was, they provided a shade for only a few minutes so it seemed, and it was a welcome relief though for only a short time. Sometimes I would watch a cloud for hours, and it seemed to never move, at least towards our field.

The Old Parker Place at Lilbert contained about 111 acres of farmland and woods. There were a number of "cross-fences" in addition to the perimeter fences. The type of fences usually depended on the crop protecting and the kind of animals and varmints wanted to keep out. Sometimes there was only a barbwire fence, some would have hog wire at the bottom, especially around the peanut field, and of course the gardens had

175

chicken wire to keep out chickens and rabbits. Posts for the fences were split from logs, and there was also a split rail cross fence near the fruit orchard. One summer when I was a bit older daddy, Ossed and I built a brush fence in a highly underbrush area, which only lasted for a year.

There was always some work to be done when the fields were too wet or didn't need cultivating. A lot of rainy and wet days were used to repair equipment and sharpen tools. Daddy had a blacksmith shop where most of this was done. It was my job to turn the "windless" (crank of the forge that kept the coal burning). Another tool in the shop was an anvil where small tools were fashioned. There were also tongs for handling hot metal, a large vise and a grinding stone for sharpening. Most of the time a bastard file was used to put a sharp edge on the "shares" and "sweeps" of the ploughs. Often times a few of the tools were removed from the shop and misplaced by me. Usually a "spanking" would refresh my memory, but not enough to prevent if from happing over and over again. I suppose that I would have carried off the anvil had it not been to big and heavy.

The girls in the family were not permitted to wear "britches" (pants and overalls) except when working in the fields. When they did wear such, it was something that belonged to one of the boys. They also had bonnets, which were hand made for working in the sun. The bonnets had slats of cardboard with a back and tail to protect the neck. They were hot and had to be removed from the head periodically as no air circulated through them. The dress code of the girls were governed by prevailing moral and religious conviction and strictly adhered to.

There was Sunday afternoons when mama, daddy, Ossed and I would walk through the field. The corn stalks were tall and green and there would be lots of cotton blooms, There would be a good "stand" of peanuts and peas. Mama and daddy would speculate on how much the crops would yield, and express hope cotton prices would be more this year. There was little doubt of them being very proud of the crops, yet they knew it was only by the "Grace of God" there would be rains with the weevils and cuts worms not destroy the crops.

All crops were harvested by hand. Peanuts were pulled up from the ground and stacked (shocked) before taking to the barn. Corn was pulled by hand from the stalks, tossed in a wagon and hauled by wagon to the crib where it was unloaded by a corn scoop. Cotton was picked by hand and placed in a sack dragged by a shoulder strip. When the wagon, with high frames, was full it would be carried to a cotton gin and sold. Men would leave early in the morning, around 3 to 4 a.m. in their wagons in order to be among the first in line. If they were late, the cotton would be ginned late and they had to return home late or spend the night in their wagons at the gin.

I remember the year daddy bought a "mule drawn" rideing cultivator. It was, of course, unassembled. Ross and daddy spent more than a day attempting to assemble it. It had two ploughs where by each side of a row could be cultivated at the same time. It was supposed to be "The Car's Meow," as opposed to ploughing one side at a time. I had never ever heard daddy curse, but he did use a few choice by-words that day. The wheels were supposed to move horizontally where by the ploughs could be positioned and kept correct in relation to the plants being cultivated. I don't think they ever got it correctly installed or lacked skill and "know how" in its use. It was short lived, and discarded as too many cotton plants were being ploughed up. Daddy may have "got it off' on someone, but most likely it remained in a pasture and eventually sold as "junk."

FOOD FOR THE 1930'S

Most of our food was grown in the fields and two gardens beside the house. Wild berry, grapes, and plums were used to make jellies and jams. Pears from three large pear trees in the orchard supplied enough pear preserves to last a year. There were years when several bushels of peaches would be "put-up" (canned) also. Sometimes the gardens didn't do well and we had to eat a lot of dried black-eye peas. The only time I allow black-eye peas in the house now is for "New Year's Day."

We always grew a "world" of Irish potatoes and "sweet tatters." Reckon I was near grown when I learned they were called yams. We ate a lot of those things, and so did the hogs. We ate them raw and usually "wound up" with a bellyache too. They were baked in the oven and often times provided the after school snack. A lot of them were pan fried and eaten, which seemed to cause a lot of gas in the stomach, which needed expelling frequently. One year a bumper crop of sweet potatoes was made and they were stored in a "dugout." Needless to say most rotted, and we were back to those darn dried peas again.

I enjoyed eating the small potatoes "grabbled" from the garden cooked with the English peas. The small potatoes would be harvested with a spoon and then cleaned with a "brush broom" as they were swished about in a number three wash tub of water. What I am about to say next has nothing to do with food of the 30's but is amusing and about small fresh Irish potatoes.

One year after being married for a while it was decided to have a garden for "old times sake." My wife hadn't been exposed to farm life much, or cooking either as a matter of fact. I sometime though she needed a recipe book for boiling water. I thought I had caught her attempting to open an egg with a can opener when we first got married. Well anyway she wanted to know if we could have some new potatoes from the garden. I told her sure we could, just grab a couple tablespoons and a pan. We went to the garden and I told her to look for cracks in the ground under the vines as potatoes would probabley be there. I was ahead of her on the row when I asked her if she was finding any. She said yes and showed me what she had in the pan. I told her they were too little and needed to grow some more. A few minutes later I looked back again and saw her pushing them back in the ground, and I asked "what are you doing?" to which she replied "you said they needed to grow some more." Folks that's not ajokel

Most of our bread was cornmeal bread and biscuits. The cornbread was made with meal from the corn we grew. Fifty pounds or more of corn would be hand shelled, or with the corn Sheller when it was working. The corn would be taken on a mule to a mill for grinding. Most of the time the pay for grinding was half of the corn taken. Sometime "store bought" cornmeal was used, and we didn't like it much. It was finer ground and had no husk in it. As I recall the mill was at Mr. Lawrence Wallace's place where he would only grind on Saturdays. Every once in a while mama would get an extra dime and buy yeast. She would bake a "pone" or two (loaf or two) of "light bread" which was a real treat.

When I was about five years old we had a wooden flour barrel which would hold a couple of fourty eight pounds sacks of flour, We dared not ever leave the lid off at night as a rat would hop in and leave notice he had been there. The flour was purchased in sacks, and the print on the sacks identifed the brand bought. Flour sacks were used to make girl's dresses and boys' shirts.

Large quantities of staples were purchased primary from Mr. Wallace at his store in Cushing. Trading was done with him as he had a better stock and better prices. Stores in the 30's had clerks that did the "clerking." That is a "bill" (list) was brought in and given to the clerk. He would take the list and fill it while other business was being attended to in town. Many store sold their "goods" on credit, and there are old ledgers today of their customers. Mama and daddy never bought on credit. If there was no money then we just "made do" until there was money.

Some weeks a grocery truck would run where we would buy "nickel and dime" things. Then sometime we would walk down to the John Whitaker store at Lilbert for a box of baking soda or a nickel tin of Garrett snuff for daddy or mama. Large quantities of staples were bought in Cushing, on a Saturday. Going to town in the wagon was an exciting time as we not only got to look in the store windows, but daddy let us drive the mules. Then when we got ready to go home daddy would buy cheese and crackers to eat on the way back. Yes, the crackers were in a cracker barrel and as many or few wanted could be bought. The cheese was big round hoop cheeses which was on a counter beside a set of scales. It probably weighed twenty pounds before any was sold from it. It was kept covered with a cloth to keep the flies off it. Some folks called it "rat cheese" as it had holes as if rats had made them. Mr. Wallace was never suspected of putting his finger on the scales while weighing out a dime's worth. Daddy often bought a dozen lemons too, and we had lemonade made with a cool bucket of well water when we got home.

I recall one such trip to Cushing made by daddy, Ossed and I, in which we had trouble on the way back. Our wagon had narrow rim wheels and the rims were prone to come off. Ossed was holding the lines that guided the mules and I was assigned the task of watching the back wheel that had a rim likely to come off, so it could be hammered back in place before it did. I didn't "pay attention" and the rim came off crushing the rest of the wheel and the axle started to drag on the ground. For a while I was fairly sure of getting a whipping or being scolded, but daddy took all in stride. He borrowed an ax from a man just down the road a way. He went into the woods and with the ax chopped down a long slender (sapling) pine pole to make repair with. A notch was cut in the large end and it rested on the front axle. The rear axle was then lifted and placed on the pole, making a slide for a wheel. The pole extended a distance rear of the wagon. The team of mules could them pull the wagon on home more easily. We were about half way home when this little mishap occurred. As the evening was drawing to close and we had not returned home mama sent an older brother, Buford, to look for us, as she was a bit worried. Daddy said later he had done this once before a long time ago when he had lost a wheel off a wagon.

When the grocery truck failed to come by for one reason or another we would buy things to "carry us" from the store at Lilbert.

I didn't like going to the store at Lilbert much without an adult along, as several people had dogs which chased kids. Once mama sent Ossed, with his friend Wayne Channel, to buy a dozen boxes of jar lids. They were told they could have any money left over to buy candy with. Ossed misunderstood, thinking that she only wanted a dozen lids bought only one box which had a dozen in it. As might be expected a lot of candy was bought and eaten. A lot of scolding took place too. They were sent back later with three or four dozen eggs to sell. It was made clear to them that all the money received was to be used of jar lids.

Daddy took the wagon every fall to a syrup mill to purchase syrup, Ossed and I were allowed to go along. It was not a bit unusual for daddy to buy twenty one-gallon buckets of Ribbon Cane Syrup, and that did not always last until the next season. The mill had two large rollers, which were close together and rolled in a horizontal plane. Stalks of cane were feed between the roller. The rollers were powered by a horse, that walked continuously in a circle. When the horse stopped, the rollers stopped and the horse had to be encouraged to keep walking. Juice that was squeezed from the stalks of cane flowed into a long trough, which was connected to a large metal vat where the juice was cooked making syrup. Usually a small metal cup hung near the trough for sampling of the juice by visitors. Some of the buckets of syrup we got would form large hunks of crystals, which we called rock candy. These had to be re-cooked on the stove to return them back to syrup.

Late fall and early winter was the time to slaughter hogs. We nearly always had a sow, which produced a litter of pigs. Sometimes there were more piglets than the sow had teats for. These would more often than not become the runts of the litter. As a young child I did not like to see our hogs slaughtered, as they were pets when they were small. We would slaughter three or four large hogs each year. This was a family event and quite often a neighbor or two would help. Neighbors were never paid, but always given a good "mess" of meat. Other close neighbors were also given a few backbones or other less desirable parts of meat even though they did not help in the process. There was always a lot of pork sausage made, and the tenderloin was the first part to be eaten, usually the day of processing. The ribs were eaten quite early also. Fat was cut away and later cooked in the OLE wash pot whereby it rendered into a lot of lard.

Lard which had been rendered from the fat pork was used as grease in cooking, and also used to make lye-soap. The meat, which had been cut into smaller pieces, was taken to the smokehouse where some might be "salted down", and some might be cured in other ways to prevent it from spoiling.

It was a night chore, usually after supper, for one of the boys to go to the smokehouse and cut a large piece meat for breakfast the next morning. If it were from a side of bacon, mama would slice it with a butcher knife and fry it for breakfast that particular morning. Sometimes we would have fried ham, butter, jellies, eggs and biscuits. Mama would make two large pans of biscuits, probably in the order of fifty biscuits each morning, I think my favorite breakfast was biscuits and gravy, as it still is today. I remember the first time we had "store bought" food for breakfast. It was a box of Post Toasties, and I thought we were truly eating "high on the hog" just like the "townies"

We nearly always had a lot of milk and butter, and they were kept down in the water well where it was cool. We were finally able to get an ice box which did a lot to improve the quality of the things needing to be kept cold. An iceman ran every day or so delivering ice to customer. We had a sign in the window, which indicated the size of ice block wanted. Usually a twenty-five pound block was bought, although there were other sizes to be had as well. Having ice also gave us the opportunity to have ice tea on Sundays, something we looked forward to a lot.

When I was quite young the milking of three or four cows was the job of the girls. As the girls married-off, milking became a chore of mine. There was only one cow to be milked then, for which I was glad. Cold milk and hot cornbread was a favorite supper meal for me. Sometime when there were a lot of eggs mama would fry three dozen or more for supper. I didn't eat eggs then, as the yellows were never well done, the way most in the family liked them. It was many years later while in the navy that I learned to eat eggs, and usually they had to be hard scrambled. The milk we had was most likely to be buttermilk that was churned in a large churn by a hand operated dasher. We also had gallons of sauerkraut each year. I suppose the things kids living on a farm dislikes the most as food is cabbage and sauerkraut.

CANNING DAYS

Most all the vegetables we ate in the 1930's, such as corn, beans, peas, tomatoes, cabbage, potatoes, okra, and squash, were "put up" (canned) at home. We also put up a lot of vegetable soup, pickles and sauerkraut. Half-gallon Mason Fruit jars were mostly used as this quantity was needed for a "bunch of hungry growing kids." Jams and jellies were usual put up in pint jars, but preserves, mostly pear, were in half-gallon jars also.

As might be expected I did not take to helping with the canning, especially when it came to shelling butter beans. They are much harder to shell than peas or pinto beans.

I suppose that I minded helping with Tomatoes the least even though there would be ten bushels to can in various ways. We always grew the tomatoes in our own tomato "patch" (field) and so were most all the other things canned that were raised by us. The tomatoes were thoroughly cleaned, pealed and precooked prior to placing them in jars and boiling them further in the large "wash pot" of water causing the lids to seal when the jars cooled.

When jars of food were emptied in preparation of a meal the jars was never rinsed out much, which necessitated a lot of scrubbing when they were used again. After a lot of washing with soap and water they had to be boiled in order to sterilize them. The cleaning of jars was one of my duties on canning days as well as keeping the fire "going" around the wash-pot. My jar cleaning did not always pass inspection and required repeat cleaning. It was not a bit unusual to get a hand scalded with the boiling water and mama would doctor it with a home remedy sometime by applying "bluing" a liquid used in the final rinse water of clothes washing. I doubt it did much good. There were times when a direct burn caused a small blister, we held it close to a fire thinking it would draw out the heat and quicken healing. There were other home remedies for other things, which were just as much ineffective and perhaps even a hindrance. One such remedy was to apply a liberty amount of "coal-oil" (kerosene) to a cut on the body.

When the canning days were over there would be a hundred jars or more lining the shelves in the smoke house where canned food was kept. There would be peas, green beans, tomatoes, vegetable soup and speckled butter beans, and quite a number of peaches pears, and berries.

Sometimes the fruit would be used in cobblers, and pies. Other times it would be eaten at breakfast, which was "powerfully good" being somewhat cool.

Pealing of peaches and pears for canning was not a job to be "fancied" however it wasn't too terrible I got to eat a little of them, especially the parts which were over ripe. Many of the major canning days followed about the same routine with various family members having simular general duties. Often times the wood burning cook stove in the kitchen was relocated outside, in the shade of a tree, as many days were very warm. We never had air conditioning, electricity, ceiling or window fans in those days either. There were also times (nights) in which I slept on the front porch on a "pallet" of quilts as it was too hot to sleep inside the house.

Probably no one was happier than I was when we commenced using cans in the majority of canning. This did not completely eliminate "jar canning" as mama did sometime continue to use a large pressure cooker, which would accommodate about one dozen half-gallon jars. Instead of me washing jars, it became my chore to seal the cans with the hand crank sealing machine. I seldom think about the "old hand sealer" without thinking of an incident in which I should have been disciplined. It just seemed like our place was "the place" for people to drop-off (leave) cats and dogs they didn't want. The people never asked if we wanted them, they would dump them unaware to us. One of the cats showed up with a litter of kittens shortly and mama commence "fussing about me" getting ride of them. The last thing she said to me that Saturday morning as she was leaving to go to Cushing was "I want that bunch of cats gone when I get back.' Mama had never said just how the cats were supposed to be gotten rid of. There were a few #3 cans left over from canning, so I place one kitten to a can and seal them, placing the cans under the house. A number of days later mama discovered the cans and in order they not be open I 'fessed-up, I don't suppose there were "tree-huggers" then and many people couldn't care less if cats were disposed of in a humane way or not. I suppose that "little stunt" wasn't considered as "meanness" which deserved a "licking" by a peach-tree limb or the belt daddy sharpened his straight blade razor on.

WASH DAYS

Washing of clothes was an activity, actually a big job, that all the kids participated in which took from early morning to late evening. Homemade lye soap was used which had been made from the fat of hogs cooked in the wash pot utilizing lye, a very poisonous powered chemical. A year supply of lye soap was generally "cooked off' not long after "hog killing day." I didn't much care for making soap either, as I had to stir it once in a while with a large wooden paddle. If there was a breeze blowing it was most important to stay ""up-wind" of the fumes given-off.

Sometimes hand soap was used if the lye soap "ran out" before the next year. This was a bar of soap by the name of P & G. They were large bars which cost five-cents each. The John Whitaker store at Lilbert, and the "rolling store' would sell six bars for a quarter. For a long time Procter and Gamble would embed a marble in the comer of the bars, The reason was obvious, and it worked as kids begged their mamas to buy their soap, even thought boys usually got a sack of marbles at Christmas.

When washing powders came to "our neck of the wood" we were reluctant to use it at first. It was referred to as "synthetic soap." As I recall we didn't "take to" margarine (oleo) when it first appeared ether. It resembled lard more than butter before the little "dap" of color was mixed with it.

Except for in the summer, wash days were on Saturday's, a day kids were not in school. A family of ten to twelve can dirty a lot of clothes in a week's time. The wash was always huge, and preparation would normally be made beforehand. Large quantities of water would be drawn from the well and three wash tubs appropriately filled took place before the actual wash day. The first tub was where the clothes were rubbed on a "rubbing board" after having been boiled in the wash pot. Wood was gathered to keep the fire around the pot and the pot was usually filled the day before as well. The other two tubs of water were for rinsing purposes. There was a person who "manned" each of the three tubs. Clothes which had been rinsed in the last tub were "hand twisted" to "ring-out" excessive water. They would then be hung on a line, which seldom ever was long enough. Many clothes were hung on fences.

When a number of the kids had left home (marrying, in the military, and away on defense work) there was no longer a labor pool of kids to help with the weekly wash. Mama sometimes hired a black lady to help when she had fifty-cents to pay her with. This black lady always brought a little girl with her, which I figure now to be about my age at the time. My guess now is that the little girl was a grandchild of hers. This black lady would not allow the little girl to speak or play with us "white folks" and kept her close by. Mama and daddy had never taught us to be prejudiced, and I could not understand then why I was not permitted to play with the little girl. The black lady probably thought mama would not like it if she didn't keep her away, and that it was just the proper way of life.

Wash days usually meant that Ossed and I had to take a bath in the last rinse water. The water was reasonably clean as all the tubs of water were replaced one or more times during the wash. We also got our heads scrubbed with lye soap too. Perhaps this was to prevent lice and dandruff, something I can never remember having. The water from the scrubbing tub and wash pot was often time used to clean the wood floors of the house.

Our water at the Old Parker Place at Lilbert wasn't the best and many times not used for washing clothes. Water was often used from a neighbors well. It was brought to our place in a barrel on a "slide" (large sled) pulled by one of the mules. Several trips would be made the day before wash day hauling several barrels of water to fill all the tubs, wash pot and have replacement water. Many years later a nephew described the water as being so hard it had to be chewed in order to swallow it.

Ovie, the oldest sibling in the family, told me a story about washing cloths, which took place when the family lived at the Old Place at Lilbert. It probably took place before I was born or when extremely young. She and some of the other girls took clothes to a well in a pasture a short distance away. There were goats in the pasture, and when Ovie put the clothes and lye soap on the ground a goat took the soap. As the story goes, Ovie chased the goat with a stick a considerable time before retrieving the soap. Another sister, Mildred once told me of this as well and still had a "good laugh" about it then even though it had happened many years in the past.

THE WAR

I do not remember much about the beginning of World War II, as I was only eleven years old. I do remember broadcasts on the radio of how the Japanese had attacked Pearl Harbor sinking a lot of ships and killing a lot of people. I had no idea who the Japanese were or had no understanding of Pearl Harbor either.

On Christmas Eve of 1941 I remember Buford, James, Ossed and myself talking of the possibility of Buford, and perhaps even daddy, having to "go to war" as we placed fire wood and "starter pine" on the from porch. This was always boys' chore who usually took turns, but I remember all were involved on this special night. We never had a wood shed at the old place but several cords of wood would be stacked a short distance from the house for the winter.

Daddy often times would walk to the country store in Lilbert, and he would let Ossed and I go with him. We were always anxious to go because after a "spell" of drooling in the candy case, daddy would buy us a peanut patty and a couple sticks of "barber-pole" candy. In was on one of these trips at the beginning of the war that daddy stopped by to speak with Mr. Nolan Whitaker. They talked at some length about the war in the shade of a big oak tree there by the road. I remember to this day that neither thought they would have to "go to war", which relieved my concern about it. They "figured" younger men, and men with small families would be "called up" (drafted) before them, and too, the war probably wouldn't last so long either.

As the war lingered on from one year to the next, we younger boys were growing up and sometimes wondered if the war would last so long we would become eligible. We had a battery-powered radio then, and almost every night the family would gather about it to listen to Gabriel Heater's newscast which he always began with "there is good news tonight" or "there is bad news tonight," We felt a special kind of pride whenever a major victory was won, but never without much sadness too when the lives lost were told. I suppose no family in America was without a relative in one of the branches of services. There were husbands, wives, sons, daughters, brothers, sisters, aunts, and uncles giving their lives for a precious God given freedom.

The people left in the states supported "the war" in every possible way. They gladly conformed to a system of rationing of many things. Women gladly "gave up" wearing silk stocking, and took on traditional men's work. Trainloads of workers arrived two times a day at shipyards and other factories. Anyone suspecte of being slack would be asked "Don't you know there is a war going on?" There was a lot of "victory gardens" grown in unexpected places, and I remember the weekly school assemblies of students where we sang a number of patriotic songs each time. The Andrew Sisters did a lot of singing to help keep people's spirit lifted. It is possible to buy their recording even to this day, which is a good reminder lest we should ever forget. The war finally came to an end in 1945 with rationing slowly going away. There were waiting lists for new cars then. More exciting was news when particular-fighting units would be reaching one of the ports. The town of Cushing planned a celebration on a Saturday just after the war and James wanted to go, but daddy didn't think it would be a good idea, perhaps fearful of the celebration "getting out of hand."

CUSHING

The small "country town" of Cushing in Nacogdoches County, like many other small towns, had very little industry, to keep it "alive." Farming sustained it in early years, as the town met most all the needs of farm life. There were fewer automobiles, with not a lot of farm people being prosperous enough to own one. Most roads were of the unimproved kind as well, which oftentimes made traveling by car impractical to larger towns.

I remember Cushing for a number of reasons. I had my first ice cream cone there, and still remember my first visit to the doctor. The visit was frightening even thought my older brother Buford, who carried me, kept assuring me there was nothing to be afraid about. Cushing was a place where a young boy could have a most enjoyable Saturday evening with "two-bits" (twenty five cents). Double feature western movies cost about 12 cents, a hamburger a dime, and a coke a nickel. It just seemed like the thing to do when going to town on Saturday to have a bowl of Chile. There was never a waitress, but a waiter (man) instead who asked what you wanted. It might be asked in an unusual way for this day and time, as he might say something like "what are you craving for?"

Mr. R.P Johnson and Mr. Frank Williams each had a "dry goods" store in Cushing. and one Saturday I had saved money and bought a pair of stripped pants and suspenders from Mr. Williams. I was one "proud dude" and wore them home. Mama took one look at me and said "young man take them stripped britches off 'cause they are going back." I begged and cried a little but mama insisted and I carried them back. As I remember Mr. Frank didn't want to take them back, but he did allow me to trade them for a much less desirable pair that seemed to please mama.

During its flourishing years Cushing could boast of having two banks, two automobile dealerships, two drug stores, two hardware stores, two general merchandise stores, two restaurants, three or more grocery stores, a bus line, two trains a day, two barber shops, a funeral home, a laundry and dry cleaning shop, a post office, with two rural routes, a feed store, a 5 & 10 cent store (racket store so called), a school, several churches, auto repair shops, several service stations, its own town Marshall and Justice of Peace. There was also a small jail for all the folks who wanted to get rowdy on Saturday night. There were two doctors, a dentist, a cotton gin and occasionally a small saw mill. There was once a small newspaper as well. Mr. "Sodie" Holsomback, owner of one of the hardware stores operated an ambulance service, and there were a couple of independent taxies as well. It is my understanding from history of the town it was started by the B & O Railroad who had a company doctor by the name of Cushing.

The growth of Cushing reached its peak in 1947, and then commenced a rapid loss of business establishments. Population decreased a little but that soon "tapered off." The population may have even increased slightly from one census taking to the next, however I never knew the population to exceed much more than nine hundred. After WWII, families who had left for defense work elsewhere came back to resume a farming life. There was little doubt they had a dislike for public work and urban living. Men returning from the war came back with dreams of starting their own businesses, and farming their lands. A few people succeeded, but the majority never "saw their dreams come true." Either they couldn't make "a go of it" or realized quickly this wasn't what they wanted to do. The people migrated to the larger towns and cities, where there were opportunities of a more fulfilling way of life.

Merchants in Cushing realized a year or so after the war was over they were losing a lot of business as people had better transportation and a desire for "things" the town could not offer. They looked for ways to stimulate business and commenced what was known as "trade days", a Saturday where there was a drawing for merchandise. Ticket was given with merchandise purchased during the week and placed inside a screen cylinder where names were drawn from. This was effective for a while, but it too suffered a loss of interest and was discontinued. The economy and population base didn't allow merchants to expand or modernize in order to be competitive with larger towns. Because the town had nothing to offer young people who finished high school in the way of public employment most left for a more promising future elsewhere.

The town of Cushing is not in 1980 as it was many years ago when I was a boy roaming the woods, and less often the streets. I go back occasionally, just to look around mostly. The streets and sidewalks once bustling with activity are deserted. A number of the old buildings, which once represented strength and stability to me, have fallen down. There is still a bank, a post office, a school and a "grocery store", but they are all in a different location. I seldom see anyone that I know or recognize, in what appeared to me as a "ghost town." I hear someone has passed on to meet their maker, and sometime about someone who has returned after a long absence, to retire or perhaps to start a small business hopeing it will be profitable enough to stay. It usually isn't, and I suppose it was more to fulfill a dream they once had. Cushing provided for a lot of good memories and I have often wished I had "tried my hand" at something there to, if for no reason other than just "the heck of it."

OUR NEIGHBORS

The Bible teaches that a neighbor is someone who helps another person in a time of need. Down through the years we have come to associate neighbors as those who live close by. This is influenced by the fact that strangers are more reluctant than ever before to help someone in need. I like to think of our neighbors while we lived at the Old Parker Place at Lilbert in the 1930's as friendly, accommodating, helpful people who lived near us. Life would have been more of a struggle to make "ends meet" had that not been so. In the country you don't just run to town to get a cup of sugar, an egg or two or a gallon of milk.

Most of the people in our community were to poor to "pay attention" or have money for "ready-rolled" cigarettes. While some of our neighbors were a little "better off' than others, they were all friendly and helpful people. We visited with a number of them quite frequently, and some hardly ever as there was not a lot in common other than being poor.

Perhaps the most prominent neighbor in the community was Mr. "Dutch" Campbell. He lived on a big place in a large house and had a large barn, which was well maintained. He owned several rent houses about and had a few "share croppers." Mr. Campbell owned a late model pick-up truck and was the only one in the community to own a tractor to farm with. He had had a previous wife, but his current wife was known to all of the kids as Ms. Georgia. Ms. Georgia was a well liked and respected in the community. She was a nice lady, accommodating and friendly. Mr. Campbell was accommodating all right, but he seemed to be a bit "grouchy" at times.

My family, and others of the community, depended on Mr. Campbell for transportation to many places. He was hired to take Mama to visit a granddaughter in Nacogdoches and one of mama's sisters in Rusk. Sometime he might be hired to haul our tomatoes and cotton to the market. He went to Cushing most every Saturday evening and people would "catch" a ride with him. He would expect ten-cents, but was often "gypped" (hoodwinked, cheated) out of pay for the ride.

The Campbell family had a female dog and there was an occasion when the dog was penned in order to keep her from copulating, when she would come into "heat." Our dog, named Trailer, kept trying to break into the pen and do what comes natural for dogs. Winnie Campbell, a daughter who sometimes appeared to be not the brightest light in the room, attempted to chase Trailer away with a broom. Trailer had something else on his mind, and he attacked Winnie and did enough damage that she had to be taken to the doctor and be sewed up in several places. Winnie was left with several large scares on her arm for the rest of her life.

Daddy just happened to be home and working in one of the fields where someone went and told him of the incident. He immediately went home, took the twelve-gage shotgun from the rack over the fireplace mantel and killed our dog.

Trailer was a gentle dog with us kids and we played with him a lot. We were sad about him being "put down", but at the same time knew it was something, which had to be done. I am sure that Mr. Campbell was more than "putout" over the matter but he never held a grudge. He apparently realized the situation for what it was.

In earlier years Mr. Campbell "ran-off" with an aunt of mine. This was something, which was not talked about in the family much. I just know that it happened. It was one of those things you didn't tell unless asked about, and I never thought it proper to ask all the "W" questions.

Mr. Campbell passed away years later after we had moved from the community, and I heard Ms. Georgia inherited a large part of the estate. According to "secondhand information" she was swindled out of her inheritance. It seems she was charmed by a "drifter" in the town that she moved to after Mr. Campbell's demise. Ms. Georgia married the man, and it wasn't long after he had got all her money that he left Ms. Georgia "high and dry" never to be heard from again

The Wilkerson family was a rather large and colorful family who lived next door, up the hill a way towards Cushing. Mr. Wilkerson had probably died before they moved there. Then again he may have been "strung up" or had just decided to "fly the coop." Several of the boys and girls were talented with string musical instruments and singing. Some of the boys would play for house dances, and some were know to take a "swig" of homebrew more that occasionally. Once we found a pile of their fruit jars and bottles across the fence on our land, and we destroyed them. Most of the boys and girls did "turn-out" to be fine respectful citizens.

Ms. Wilkerson married a neighbor who was a widower. They moved out of the community with an old pick-up truck loaded down with furnishing and some small kids. A fifteen-year-old girl was left on the doorsteps crying her "eye balls out" so I am told. We never know about these kinds of things, and back then it was no ones business except theirs. Perhaps there just wasn't enough room in the truck for her. She got married at a very young age to a good man, and according to all accounts it has been a happy marriage.

If there ever was a godly person that would have to be Mrs. Huffman Channel. Don't know if I ever knew her given name. All of us kids referred to her as "Sister Channel", as she was a "Lay Apostolic' minister. Prayer was as much of Sister Channel's daily life as getting up in the morning. The family had moved into the house next to us where the Wilkerson family had lived. Sister Channel usually went in the woods behind her house to pray, and she could be heard an "axle greasing" away praying for the salvation of her family. She was truly a transparent person in this respect and "poured her heart" out to the Lord daily, and sometime more often. The best I can "reck-co-lect" (recollect) Mr. Channel never took up with religion and remained a pompous cantankerous arrogant "old fart." Well, we can hope that he did repent of his wayward life style. He really wasn't all "bad" as he "pretty well" carried Sister Channel to church regularly and kept employed. Wayne Channel, a son of theirs was a good play friend to Ossed, my youngest brother.

Another family, which once lived in the same house for a "spell", was Walter and Ruth Hodge. As it was before the Wilerson and Channel families I only remember a few things concerning them and that would be mostly Ruth. Ruth was considered to be a worldly kind of person. She was probably referred to as a "hussy", what ever that is, and a "Jezebel" because she wore "pan cake" make up, rouge and lipstick that Tammy Fay, you know who, couldn't hold a candle too. (You younger folks that mean there was no comparison and Ruth held the Guinness Book record.) Ruth wore "bob-tail" (short) hair, and a few years ahead of the times with miniskirts. She wore erring, bracelets and other "ornaments." She probably smoked and wore shorts too, making her someone "respectful women" would shun and not associate with. Ruth had a dressing table in her bedroom where she kept "worlds" of face "powder and paint." One day when she was away, Ossed and I went into her bedroom and had a jolly good time with smearing it around on the mirror, vanity and floor. Ruth suspected who the culprits were, came to the house with a most angry disposition, and gave mama a good piece of her mind. (She probably had some to spare, that is "mind") Needless to say Ossed and I paid for that little escapade in hide with a peach tree limb switching.

We had some neighbors, of sort who lived at a place that we rented later. I will not mention names which will be for obvious reasons.

There were two small girls in this family who came to our house occasionally to play with us. We were never permitted to go to their house to play. Mama felt the girls had to be watched closely as they were known to take things, and she didn't want them coming around. She was to learn there were other reason too. Their visits would be a complete waste of time if they were not able to slip something under their dresses and leave with it.

One year at the Lilbert Community Easter Egg Hunt, one of the older girls found a nest of eggs. To make a long story short, the girl had on "bloomers" (short under pants, with long legs designed to fit tight about the legs), and couldn't resist taking them. As the story goes, it was a nest, which had been abandon, with all the eggs rotten. According to a sister, which I also will not name, this girl could not resist taking them and put them in her bloomers. She was said to have been quite odorous during the walk back home.

Being a naive farm boy I had little knowledge, or education concerning the "birds and bees." One could not help see a bull mounting a cow or a rooster a chicken. Kids such as me were not terribly concerned about the "why" of it either. I might add that pregnant women were very discreet and seldom left their homes except for "have to" cases. In fact some women were so modest they would place their under clothing inside another garment for hanging on a line outside the house for drying.

Mama became a bit "upset" and shocked when I asked her about one of the girls wanting to go play "pussy" in the cottonseed out in the old car shed. I don't know just what took place to prevent it, but the girls didn't come back anymore to play.

Annie Mae Pierce and her brother Ray lived in the house Daddy had built for Aunt Callie to live in. It was a time later when the house had been moved a distance away on the road to Cushing. Near the Prince Place. I was told that Uncle Henry once lived there as well at this new location, Ray wasn't afraid of work and sometime he could be found asleep in the field where he was supposed to plough, usually in the shade of a tree, Annie Mae "kept house" for the family and went to high school. Mr. Pierce didn't have a wife and I never knew why.

Many mornings Annie Mae would still have her apron on when she boarded the school bus. She had to "grab" her books and make a dash for the bus, but I doubt the bus driver would have left without knowing for sure she wasn't going those days. Annie May was a very determined person about school, but her work of preparing breakfast for the family demanded the "last minute" at home. The Pierces lived in our neighborhood during the time Ovie returned home after finishing Bible College. Ovie thought we needed a revival in the community and decided to hold a "brush arbor" meeting. The boys "fixed" the "brush arbor" meeting place in front of the house across the road and all the kids in the neighborhood were invited. Ovie was a strong believer of people getting the "baptism" as a sign of receiving salvation of the Lord. Several kids did come, Ovie preached and had an "alter call" each time. One time Annie Mae came forward and knelt at the alter while she was being prayed for. As I recall Ovie was determined for Annie Mae to get the "baptism" as there was a lot praying, pounding on her back. The evening grew on and service was finally dismissed. The next day someone asked Annie Mae if she got the "baptism" last night. She said no she didn't think so, but she sure get a sore back from the meeting. You had to have known Annie Mae, and been there to appreciate the way she replied. Annie Mae and Ray did not go with their dad when he "hook-up" with the Wilkerson woman and moved away. Many years later one of my older sisters met Annie Mae again. She had finished high school, went on to collage and received a degree in nursing and was a supervisor at a hospital. Annie Mae is a "success story" of a highly disadvantaged person who possessed determination to "pull herself up by her own boot straps" so to speak.

Ineather Barnhart was several years older than I was and she was a very beautiful girl. She was blind, but had not been blind always. As a younger girl she had accidentally got lye in her eyes which caused blindness. Ineather lived with her Mother and Dad just a few houses "up the road" from us. She with her Mother came to visit us often. I think everyone in the neighborhood was very fond of Ineather, not because of being blind but she was a sweet lovely person. We were all sad when one day they came and said they were. moving away from the community. A year or so later Ineather came back to see us again. She was not the same person, as we had known her. This time she was happier than ever.

Ineather's new husband came with her when she came to visit us. I remember being very proud of her because I don't think I had ever seen two people happier. I'm not sure if we ever heard from her again after this visit. It was sort of hard to keep "track" of folks in those days.

Lonnie and Jackie Smith lived in the house that was in the bend (curve) of the road, which was next to us towards Lilbert. Jackie was the daughter of Mr. "Dutch" Campbell by his first wife. Jackie was a good woman and wanted to be sociable and friendly. Lonnie didn't take to being sociable much. He often caught me in his plum orchard when I slipped in it and he would chase me out. Seems to me he always had an evil eye out for me.

The Tuller family moved into Lonnie and Jackie's place after they moved away. They had a son and daughter, Herbert and Lottie who were about Buford's age. Herbert sort of looked after me like a brother. He was drafted in the army not long after they had moved into the community. Lottie was a pretty girl and I think Buford may have dated her once or twice. I used to slip off down to their house in the late evening and sit on their porch and talk a spell with them.

The J.T. Self family moved into the house that the Barnharts had lived it. They had kids about our age, a boy name Eual Dean, and a daughter named Karla "Carl" Ruth. There was also a younger son named Max. J. T was a cousin to mama. He was a industrious kind of person, always working at one thing or another when not farming. I remember he once came by the house with several other men on their way to cut pulpwood. Ms. Louise, J.T's wife, was just as industrious. It was said she didn't have a lazy bone in her. She could pick more cotton than most men. She would leave the cotton patch about mid-morning, go fix lunch and bring it to the field for her family. She nearly always brought a gallon jug of ice tea.

Another family lived in the house after the Selfs by the name of Case. They had a daughter a year or two older than I who was very "homely looking." There was a boy a year or so older than I named Louie who was a bit "unsavory" and "uncouth" as well. Mama didn't like him coming around and us playing together. Mama had a real knack for "knowing" people. We did get into mischievous things a bit.

There was a family by the name of *"so and so"* who lived several houses away from us on the road to Cushing. There was a boy in the family who was about the age of my twin sisters, and I think they wanted to date him, and may have on the "sly." The boy was very likeable and neat but there was our daddy who "stood in the way." The man of the house couldn't see very well and it was "neighborhood gossip" of his wife "stepping out" on him. She would come by our house walking and very soon a man would come by, the woman would get in his car and they would drive away. Course giving her a ride each time could have been just a coincidental meeting and that's all there was to it.

The Homer King family lived down the lane and across the woods from us. Like the Albert Bettis family, their children were grown when I was a small boy. Once daddy sent Buford, an older brother, over to Mr. King's house to borrow his ax. Daddy had broken the handle of his and didn't want to take the time to fashion another one. Mr. King sent word back to Daddy that he didn't lend his ax. A week or so later Mr. King sent someone over to our house to borrow our crosscut saw. Daddy sent word back that he didn't lend his crosscut saw. Mr. King got the message and came over immediately and apologized. From that time afterwards they lent and borrowed from each other. The Kings had a daughter name Ethel who was married to a Mixon. Ethel stayed at her parent's home a lot. I liked Ethel a lot as a kid, probably more like adored her. When I would wander over to their place Ethel would give me cookies and fruit juice. I think she would have like to have had a little boy to do things for. I don't know if they every did have any children, but probabley did, and if so I hope they had a boy.

To my knowledge there were never any neighbors who were at "odds" with each other. I suppose times were just too hard and families depended upon each other a bit too much to get "peeved" over matters that people of this day do. It is nice to be "well to do" and a little independent but it is nicer to be poor and dependent. It wasn't necessary to lock up things in the 1930's. Neighbors looked after each other's kids, and might even give them a spanking once in a while if needed. People penned each other's live stock when they broke out of the pasture and didn't steal from each other.

I often wonder what is the real cause for all the turmoil and things being the way they are in the 1980's and just what it would be like if everyone would be a neighbor like the country folks in our community in the 1930's.